Illustrated Stories That Model Psychological Skills

Joseph Strayhorn, Jr.

Illustrated by Catherine Fischer, Laura Kratochvila, Alice Schaeffer, James Brown, Michelle Vennare, and Jillian Strayhorn

Psychological Skills Press

Wexford, Pennsylvania

Copyright © Joseph Strayhorn, 2003

Published by
Psychological Skills Press
263 Seasons Drive, Wexford, PA 15090
www.psyskills.com

Author's email: joestrayhorn@juno.com.

Second printing, February 27, 2005

Thanks to Jean Fritsch for scanning the pictures, typing the captions, and retouching art work.

The plot of "The Man and the Lion" is credited to Aesop.

Illustration Credits: Artists and first pages of stories they illustrated:
Catherine Fischer:
30,33,36,38,55,72,74,83,89,99,130,137,140,144,150,153,156,165,168,171,176,181,194, 197,200,205,209,215,220,224,233,237,240,243,246,250,254,261,264,268,271,274,277, 280,283,288,293,295,299,305,318
Laura Kratochvila: 7,10,13,15,21,24,43,46,49,59,67,80,107,114,125,133,161
Alice Shaefer: 18,41,52,62,86,96,105,111,185,188,191,228
James Brown: 27,64,77,92,122,158
Michelle Vennare: 102,118,127,147
Jillian Strayhorn: 70
Cover Drawing by Jillian Strayhorn

ISBN: 1-931773-08-4

Contents

Introduction 6
Sheila Gives the Money Back 7
Jack Pets the Dog 10
Toby Plays with a Lonesome Boy 13
Timmy and Matthew Take Turns 15
Larry Keeps Sitting 18
Don Helps His Mother 21
Mary Had a Good Time Anyway 24
Rusty Forgives Lunk 27
Eddie Helps Maureen 30
Bill Ignores Clint 33
Bill Shares the Banana 36
Jerry Helps the Child Out of the Water 38
James Helps Clara 41
Cathy Says Something Nice 43
Gwen Helps Jimmy 46
Myrna Helps the Boy Get Some Water 49
Gina Helps Nancy 52
Brian Plays with Puppets 55
Sherry Shares Her Doll 59
Ted Gives His Seat to an Old Man 62
Rusty Helps Push Cars 64
Zeke Helps the Boys Fly the Kite 67
Rusty Fixes the Boy's Bicycle 70
Gina Helps Her Dog 72
Tony and Diane 74
Jane Gives a Greeting Card 77
Richard Helps Michael 80
Helen and the Strawberries 83
Amy Doesn't Let What People Say Bother Her 86
Alex Lets Jimmy Ride on the Bicycle 89
Rusty Helps Tommy Learn to Swim 92
Margo Feeds the Birds 96
Charlie Helps His Brother 99
Louis Fastens the Seat Belt 102

The Witch and the Wizard Talk Out Their Problem 105
Hank Doesn't Get to Go to the Zoo 107
Kenny and Jerry and the Alligators 111
Jan Tells Her Brother a Story 114
Linda Takes Care of Her Baby Doll 118
Jason Tames the Horse 122
Maurice Shows a Book to a New Boy 125
Jean Comforts Her Baby Sister 127
The Boy and the Video Machines 130
Michael Gives Back the Magic Wand 133
Larry and the Monkey 137
The Man and the Lion 140
Mr. Monster Helps Mrs. Monster 144
Lucia Helps Her Mother Change the Baby's Diapers 147
Helen and Her Brother 150
Brian Sees the Glove 153
Teddy and His Resting Mother 156
Rusty Helps Timmy Fetch His Dog 158
Lester Helps the Jumping Elf 161
Maggie and Mrs. Robinson 165
Joe and Larry Get the Tree 168
James Lind Does and Experiment 171
Jack Saves the Man from Freezing 176
Jack Helps the People Keep Warm 181
Paul Reads to His Mother 185
Gina Forgives Her Brother 188
Mack Helps the Little Girl 191
Jimmy and Rolf-Ola Uglyzit 194
Frank Stops to Think 197
The Boy Goes to the Amazing People's Party 200
The Girl Waits for the Deer 205
Hal and the Contest at the Magic Kingdom 209
Marilyn Becomes Friends with a Lonely Girl 215
The Amazing Person Helps Amos Not To Break Things 220
Amos Stops to Think 224
Deborah Helps the Squirrel 228
Harry Helps His Dog 233
The Boy and the Complicated Present 237
The Boy and the Rattlesnake 240

Jeff and the Broken Cup 243
Sheila Gets Separated From Her Mother 246
Gina and the Gymnastics Meet 250
Alex Helps the Animals 254
The Girl Handles it When Her Friend Leaves 261
Jean Handles It When Patty Moves Away 264
Frank and Zane Go Running 268
Freddy and the Explosive 271
James Lets the Little Boy Play With the Basketball 274
George and the One-Way Street 277
Judy Makes a Plan About Her Dog 280
Peter and His Grandmother 283
The Boy and His Bow and Arrows 288
The Boy and the Football 293
Ted Waits for His Friends to Finish Playing 295
The Boy Who Could Put Up With His Parents' Paying Attention to Something Else 299
The Boy Learns About Champions' Mistakes 305
Cindy and the Scary Bedtime Problem 318
Appendix: Using These Stories to Teach Sixteen Skills and Principles 335

Introduction

Productivity, joyousness, kindness, honesty, fortitude, good decisions, nonviolence, respectful talk.... these and others are the qualities that make lives better. These are the habits I refer to as "psychological skills."

How do young children learn these psychological skills? The models, the examples they see, are very important. And part of the way that children get positive models is through stories. The young child needs many, many concrete examples of all psychological skills. The more positive examples are stored in the child's memory bank, the more those positive patterns will be available when the child makes choices about what to do.

The stories in this book are meant to be positive models. Almost all of them are without violence and without "villains." They are constructed with the psychological development of young children as the first priority, and with entertainment value as second priority. Yet it has been very gratifying to me how many children have enjoyed these stories greatly, and have wanted to hear them over and over. This is especially true when the stories are read with great enthusiasm and energy. I hope that they will provide many hours of pleasant time for an adult and a child sitting and reading together.

It's also fun to use these stories in classrooms. You can put them on overhead transparencies and read them to a group of children. Sometimes the children enjoy answering the question, "What did someone do that was smart or good in that story?"

Another fun way to use these stories with groups of children is to act them out. You pick someone to be each character. Someone reads the story, stopping after each panel to let the actors act out what was just read. Alternatively, you read the whole story and then act it out, without refreshing the memory about what happens next.

Another way to use these stories is as models for "homemade modeling stories" that you create. When a child does something smart or good or imitation-worthy, you write down the story of what happened, with a sentence or two on each page. You draw some pictures or let the child draw some pictures to illustrate. You staple the story down the sides, and you now have another illustrated modeling story. A growing pile of homemade illustrated modeling stories is a great gift to any child, from parent or teacher.

Sheila Gives the Money Back

One time, there was a girl named Sheila.

Sheila saw a woman. The woman dropped something. Sheila saw what happened.

The woman walked away. She didn't know she had dropped something.

Illustrated Stories that Model Psychological Skills

Sheila Gives the Money Back

The woman said, "Thank you! You really helped me! That was nice of you."

Sheila felt good.

Illustrated Stories that Model Psychological Skills

Jack Pets the Dog

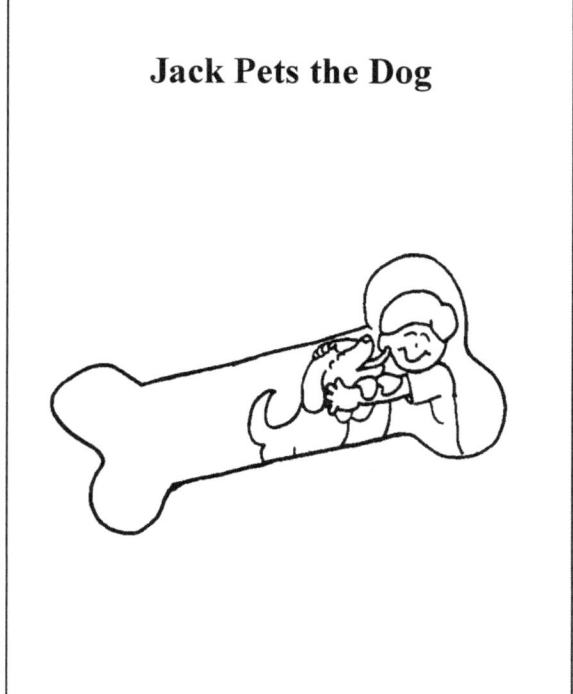

One time there was a boy named Jack.

Jack was outside.

Jack was eating a sandwich.

Jack Pets the Dog

A little dog came to Jack. Jack recognized the dog. The dog belonged to a man Jack knew.

Jack gave the dog a piece of his sandwich.

The dog liked the food. Jack felt good.

Then Jack petted the dog.

Illustrated Stories that Model Psychological Skills

And then he petted him some more.

The dog's owner came to them. He said, "Hi, Jack. I'm glad you like my dog."

The man said, "I like for people to be kind to my dog. You can play with him some more."

The man and the dog went away. Jack felt good that he had been kind to the dog.

Toby Plays with a Lonesome Boy 	One time there was a boy named Toby. Toby was on a playground. 
Toby saw another boy. This boy looked lonesome. 	Toby thought, "He looks lonesome. Maybe I can cheer him up." 

Illustrated Stories that Model Psychological Skills

So Toby said to the boy, "Do you want to play on the swings with me?"

Toby said, "You can swing, and I'll push you."

The teacher saw them having fun.

The teacher said, "Good playing, boys."

Timmy and Matthew Take Turns

Once there was a boy named Timmy. Timmy and Matthew both wanted to play on the swing.

Timmy said, "I wanted to swing. Did you want that too?"

Matthew said, "Yes. What do you think we should do?"

Illustrated Stories that Model Psychological Skills

Timmy said, "I've got an idea. Let's take turns. First you swing and I'll push. Then it will be my turn to swing."

So Timmy pushed Matthew in the swing.

Then it was Timmy's turn to swing.

The teacher said, "Good for you, Timmy and Matthew. You took turns!"

Timmy and Matthew Take Turns

Timmy felt good.

Illustrated Stories that Model Psychological Skills

Larry Keeps Sitting

Once there was a boy named Larry.

The teacher told the children to sit down.

Then the teacher said, "Please keep sitting down."

Larry Keeps Sitting

Then the teacher went to do something else.

After a while, some of the children got up.

Then more of them got up.

Larry started to get up too. But he remembered what the teacher had said.

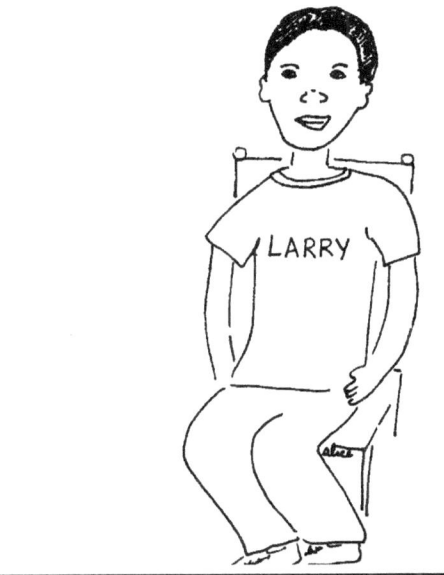

Illustrated Stories that Model Psychological Skills

So he kept sitting.

The teacher came back.

The teacher said, "You did what I asked you to! You're the only ones who did! I'm pleased with you!"

Larry felt good.

Don Helps His Mother

One time there was a boy named Don.

Don's mother was carrying some things.

Don said, "May I help you carry these things?"

Illustrated Stories that Model Psychological Skills

Don's mother said, "Yes, please, Don."

So, Don helped his mother carry the books and boxes.

Finally, they finished their job.

Don's mother said, "Thanks Don! You're a good helper!"

Don Helps His Mother

Illustrated Stories that Model Psychological Skills

Mary Had a Good Time Anyway

Once there was a girl named Mary.

She was at home.

Mary's mother was getting supper ready.

Mary Had a Good Time Anyway

Mary said, "Mama, may I put on some music and dance around?"

Mary's mother said. "Not now, Mary. It's almost time to eat."

Mary said, "OK. That doesn't bother me."

Mary's mother said, "I like what you just did. I said No, and you did what I told you. And you didn't let it bother you."

Illustrated Stories that Model Psychological Skills

Rusty Forgives Lunk

People knew that Rusty was the strongest person around.

Alex said to Lunk, "I dare you to say something nasty to Rusty."

Lunk went up to Rusty and said something very mean and nasty. Then he started to run away.

Illustrated Stories that Model Psychological Skills

But, Rusty was also very quick. He grabbed Lunk and said, "Wait a minute."

People wondered what Rusty would do to Lunk.

But Rusty said, "I just wanted to forgive you for what you said to me."

Alex said, "Rusty, I dared him to do it. It's really my fault."

Rusty Forgives Lunk

Rusty said, "I forgive you too."

Rusty thought to himself, "I'm glad I was kind to those boys." And he felt good. People looked at Rusty and said, "He's a good man."

Illustrated Stories that Model Psychological Skills

One time there was a boy named Eddie.

Eddie and his friends were on the playground.

It was a cold day. Eddie's friend Maureen was cold.

Eddie Helps Maureen

Eddie was very warm. He had on a big sweater and a heavy coat.

Eddie said, "Maureen, would you like to wear my coat?"

Maureen said, "Thanks, Eddie. That's really nice of you."

Now Maureen wasn't cold anymore.

Bill Ignores Clint

One time there was a boy named Bill.

The teacher said, "It's time for free play."

A boy named Clint came up and pushed Bill.

Illustrated Stories that Model Psychological Skills

Bill thought, "He's just trying to get to me. I won't let him do that. I won't pay any attention to him."

Bill walked away and started to work on a puzzle.

Clint kept trying to get to Bill. He knocked a piece of the puzzle off the table.

Bill said to himself, "I can stay cool."

Bill Ignores Clint

Clint went away.

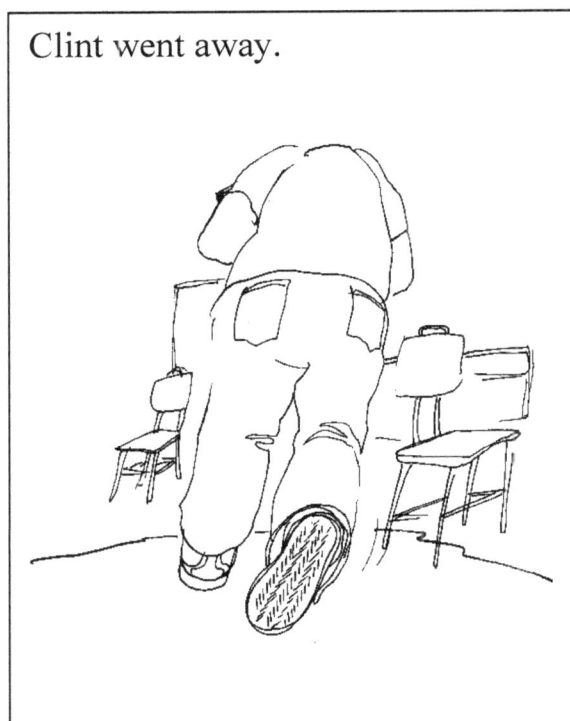

The teacher said, "Good for you, Bill! You stayed cool! You didn't let him bug you."

Bill felt good.

Illustrated Stories that Model Psychological Skills

Bill Shares the Banana

One time there was a boy named Bill.

Bill had a banana to eat.

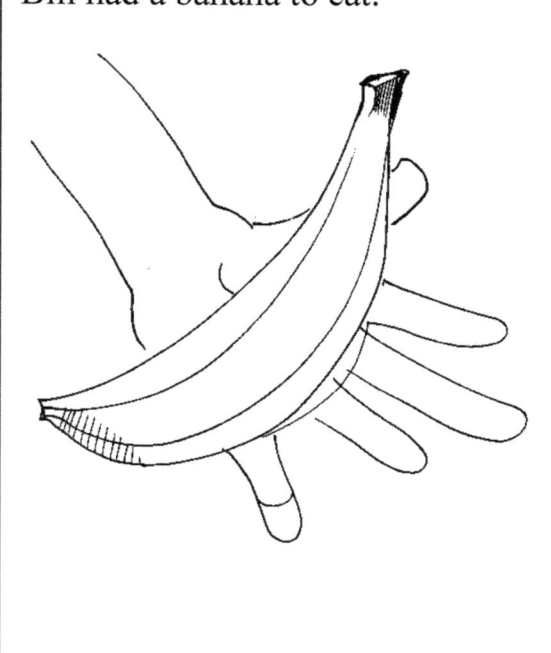

Bill saw his friend Pete. Pete said, "Hi Bill!"

Bill Shares the Banana

Bill said, "Hi, Pete! Glad to see you!"

Bill said, "Would you like some of my banana?"

Pete said, "Thank you, Bill!" He took some of the banana.

Bill felt good because he had made Pete happy.

Illustrated Stories that Model Psychological Skills

Jerry Helps the Child out of the Water

Jerry was at a park. There was a fountain at the park.

A very little boy was playing near the fountain. He was reaching for a leaf in the water.

All of a sudden the little boy fell in the water. Jerry saw what happened.

Jerry Helps the Child Out of the Water

Jerry ran as fast as he could to help the boy. 	Jerry hopped into the water to get the boy. 
Jerry lifted the little boy out of the water. 	The little boy's parents ran to where they were. 

Illustrated Stories that Model Psychological Skills

The mother took the little boy. The father said, "Thanks, young man."

Jerry said, "You're welcome." Jerry felt good because he knew that he had probably saved the little boy from drowning.

James Helps Clara

Clara was a fire-breathing dragon.

One day, Clara got sick.

She tried to breathe out some flames, but since she was sick, her flame-maker wouldn't work.

Illustrated Stories That Model Psychological Skills

Clara had a friend named James who happened to be another dragon. Clara said, "James, could I use your flame? Mine isn't working because I'm sick." James said, "Sure, Clara, I'll be glad to help."

So James lit the fire for Clara. Clara said, "Thanks, James."

After that, Clara invited James to stay for lunch. They had fun.

Cathy Says Something Nice

Cathy Says Something Nice

One time there was a girl named Cathy.

One morning Cathy was at school.

Cathy's friend Angie came to the school.

Illustrated Stories That Model Psychological Skills

Angie had been gone for a few days. Cathy was glad Angie was back.

Cathy said, "I'm glad you're back, Angie. I missed hearing your good ideas! And I missed seeing your nice smile!"

Angie said, "Thank you, Cathy. That's nice of you to say that. I missed you, too."

The teacher heard them. She said, "What nice things you two are saying! I love it when my students are nice to each other!"

Cathy Says Something Nice

Illustrated Stories That Model Psychological Skills

Gwen Helps Jimmy

One time there was a girl named Gwen.

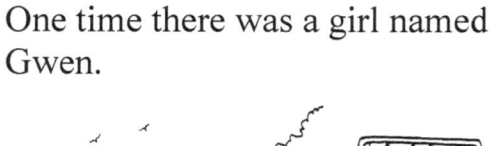

A little boy named Jimmy was also at the park.

All of a sudden a big dog started barking at Jimmy.

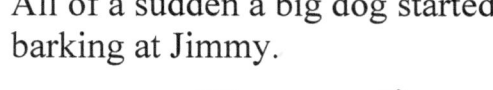

Gwen Helps Jimmy

Gwen ran to Jimmy.

Gwen picked Jimmy up in her arms.

Gwen said, "Leave us alone, dog."

Gwen said, "Don't worry, Jimmy. He won't bother us."

Illustrated Stories That Model Psychological Skills

Jimmy's mother came to them. She said, "Thanks, Gwen. You really helped us out."

The dog's owner put the dog on a leash. He said, "I'm sorry my dog scared your son."

Jimmy's mother said, "He wasn't scared for very long, thanks to Gwen, here."

Soon Jimmy was having fun again. Gwen felt good that she had helped him.

Myrna Helps the Boy Get Some Water

Myrna Helps the Boy Get Some Water

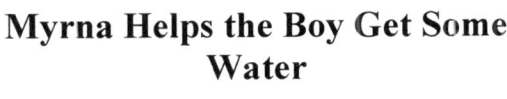

Once there was a girl named Myrna.

It was very hot outside.

Myrna drank from the water fountain. The cool water tasted good.

Illustrated Stories That Model Psychological Skills

Myrna started to walk away.

But then Myrna saw a little boy. He wanted some water. But he wasn't big enough to get it.

Myrna said, "Would you like me to lift you up?" The boy said, "Yes, please."

So Myrna lifted up the boy. That way he could drink the water.

Myrna Helps the Boy Get Some Water

The boy said, "Thank you, Myrna. I was really thirsty. That water tasted good."

Myrna said, "You're welcome." She felt good that she had been able to help him.

Illustrated Stories That Model Psychological Skills

Gina Helps Nancy

Once there was a girl named Gina.

Gina saw a girl named Nancy. Nancy didn't know how to tie her shoes yet.

Nancy's shoes kept coming off.

Gina Helps Nancy

Nancy also sometimes tripped over her shoelaces.

Gina said, "Would you like me to tie your shoes, Nancy?"

Nancy said, "Yes, please, that would be very nice of you, Gina!"

Gina tied Nancy's shoes. She showed Nancy how to do it, so that someday Nancy could tie her own shoes.

Illustrated Stories That Model Psychological Skills

Now Nancy's shoes didn't come off, and she didn't trip.

Gina felt good because she had made Nancy happy.

Brian Plays With Puppets

Brian Plays With Puppets

Once there was a boy named Brian.

Brian had a friend named C.J.

Brian said to C.J., "Do you want to play with these puppets?"

Illustrated Stories that Model Psychological Skills

Brian Plays With Puppets

C.J. said, "I need to get over to that other wall. May I ride on your back while you jump over there?"

Brian said, "Sure! Here we go."

C.J. said, "Thank you, Mr. Frog."

Brian said, "You're welcome, Mr. Spider."

Illustrated Stories that Model Psychological Skills

Brian had a good time playing with puppets.

Sherry Shares Her Doll

Sherry Shares Her Doll

One time there was a girl named Sherry. Sherry had a doll.

Sherry saw her friend Alice. She said, "Hi, Alice."

Alice said, "Hi, Sherry. How are you doing?"

Illustrated Stories That Model Psychological Skills

Sherry thought, "Alice likes to pretend. Maybe she would like to play with me now."

Sherry said, "Would you like to play with my doll with me?"

Alice said, "Yes! We can make up some plays together."

They made up lots of plays. They used their minds to have fun.

Sherry felt good because she knew she was helping her friend Alice have a good time.

Ted Gives His Seat to an Old Man

Ted got onto the bus.

At first, there were plenty of seats.

But more and more people got on the bus, and all the seats were taken.

Ted Gives His Seat to an Old Man

Then an old man got on the bus.

Ted said to the man, "You can have my seat, sir."

The man said, "Thank you, son. That's a big help to me."

Ted felt good that he had been able to help the man.

Illustrated Stories That Model Psychological Skills

Rusty Helps Push Cars

Once there was a boy named Rusty. He exercised every day.

One day it snowed a lot.

The streets were slippery. Cars were getting stuck.

Rusty Helps Push Cars

Rusty said, "Would you like a push?"

Rusty pushed the car.

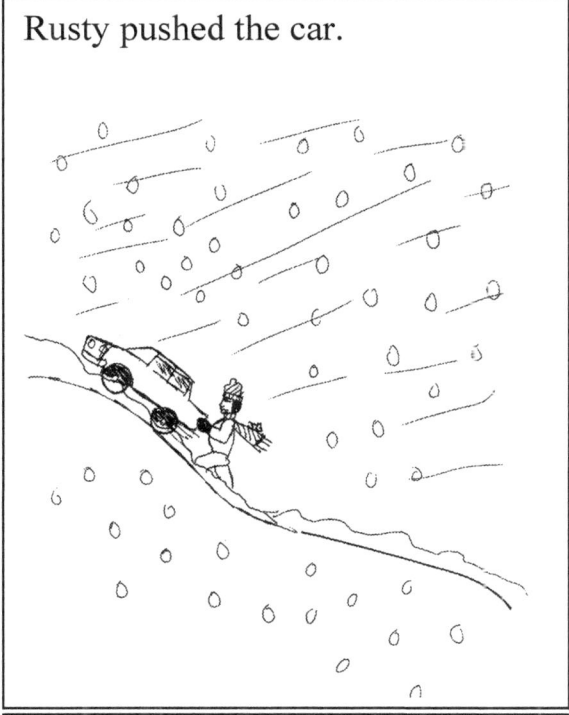

The driver was very happy. She yelled, "Thanks, Rusty!"

Rusty kept pushing more cars...

Illustrated Stories That Model Psychological Skills

...and more cars.

Rusty was tired, but he felt good because he had helped so many people.

Zeke Helps the Boys Fly the Kite

Once there was a boy named Zeke. He was in the park.

Zeke saw boys trying to fly a kite.

The kite kept falling down. The boys couldn't get it to fly.

Illustrated Stories That Model Psychological Skills

Zeke knew a lot about kites. Zeke said, "May I help you?" A boy said, "Sure. If you know how to get it to fly, we can use some help."

Zeke said, "The kite needs a longer tail. And the string needs to be tied on a little higher."

Zeke said, "Now try it. I bet it will fly now."

The boys tried again to fly the kite.

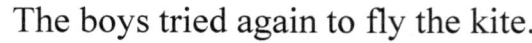

Zeke Helps the Boys Fly the Kite

This time it worked!

One of the boys said, "Thanks for helping us!"

Zeke said, "You're welcome!" Zeke felt good that he had been able to help.

Illustrated Stories That Model Psychological Skills

Rusty Fixes the Boy's Bicycle

Rusty was jogging.

Rusty saw a boy with a bicycle. The bicycle wasn't working.

Rusty said, "Would you like some help with your bike?"
The boy said, "Yes, please."

Rusty Fixes the Boy's Bicycle

Rusty worked on the bike.

Rusty said, "Now try it. I think it'll work now."

The boy said, "It works now! Thanks, Rusty!"

Rusty said, "You're welcome!" He felt good that he had been able to help the boy.

Gina Helps Her Dog

Gina had a dog named King.

One night, King came home with a big burr in his hair. A burr is a big, prickly seed that grows on certain plants and will stick on people's clothes or in animals' hair.

When Gina saw this burr, she said to herself, "That burr will probably hurt King when he lies down. I want to help him by taking it off. But how can I do that without pulling his hair?"

Gina Helps Her Dog

Then Gina said to herself, "I know. I'll take a clump of hair and hold it still, and then I'll pull the burr out while I'm holding the hair. That way I won't hurt King."

So Gina pulled the burr out, just the way she had planned.

King looked happy. Gina thought, "I bet he likes that better."

Gina felt good that she had been able to help King.

Illustrated Stories That Model Psychological Skills

Tony and Diane

One time there were a brother and a sister named Tony and Diane.

They were getting ready to watch a TV show.

Tony said, "I want to watch Mr. Rogers' Neighborhood."

Tony and Diane

And Diane said, "Oh -- I want to watch the cartoons, and they come on at the same time."

So for a while neither of them could decide what to do.

Finally Diane said, "I'll tell you what. You've done a lot of nice things for me lately, so I'll let you watch your show. I'll watch with you, or do something else if I don't like it."

Tony said, "Thanks, Diane. You're really a nice sister."

Illustrated Stories That Model Psychological Skills

Diane felt good because she had been able to make her brother feel good.

Jane Gives a Greeting Card

Jane Gives a Greeting Card

A husband and a wife had a big argument with each other.

The woman went outside for a walk.

It was the holiday season, but the woman did not feel happy.

Jane thought, "That woman looks sad. I wonder what I can do to make her happier. I know, I'll give her a greeting card."

Jane wrote a nice card for the woman.

Here is what the card looked like.

Jane gave the card to the woman just before Jane got on the bus. She said to the woman, "This is for you. Have a nice night!"

Jane Gives a Greeting Card

Jane could see that the card made the woman feel good. So, Jane felt good herself.

The woman went home and showed the card to her husband.

They felt better now, and they sat down to work out their problems in a nice way.

Illustrated Stories That Model Psychological Skills

Once there was a boy named Richard.

Richard and Michael were outside drawing some pictures.

They were drawing with colored pencils. Michael put his pencil down to go and look at Richard's picture.

Richard Helps Michael

All of a sudden a bunch of boys came running by.

One of the boys stepped on Michael's pencil.

Michael's pencil was broken so badly that he couldn't use it. Michael said, "Now I can't finish my picture."

Richard said, "Would you like to use my pencil, Michael?"

Illustrated Stories That Model Psychological Skills

Michael said, "Yes, please. That's nice of you, Richard."

They found another place to draw. Michael finished his picture.

When they were both through drawing, they looked at each other's pictures.

Richard felt good that he had helped his friend.

Helen and the Strawberries

Helen and the Strawberries

Once upon a time, there was a girl named Helen. Helen and her sister loved to have fresh strawberries to eat.

They both would ask their mother, "Mama, please bring home some strawberries for us from the store."

Their mother said, "Fine, I will."

Illustrated Stories That Model Psychological Skills

Their mother went out and did her many chores. That evening they had supper and Helen said, "Oh, I can't wait for dessert, because it is strawberries!"

Then their mother said, "Oh, I forgot to get them when I was out. I'm sorry."

Helen's sister started to whine and complain. She said, "But you promised! Why didn't you remember?"

But Helen thought to herself, "Well, I can't have everything I want just when I want it."

And to her mother she said, "Oh, that's OK. Maybe we can get some another day soon. Everybody forgets things."

Helen's mother seemed to feel good when Helen said this.

Helen thought to herself, "I'm glad I was able to put up with not getting my way and still stay in a good mood."

Illustrated Stories That Model Psychological Skills

Amy Doesn't Let What People Say Bother Her

Amy was a hippopotamus. One day she was going for a walk.

One of the giraffes said to the other, "I think she's too fat, don't you?"

Amy thought, "Let's see. Are they right in what they are saying about me? I don't think so. I don't think I'm too fat for a hippopotamus."

Amy Doesn't Let What People Say Bother Her

So Amy didn't give another thought to what they had said.

One snake said to the other, "I think her skin is too saggy, don't you?" Amy heard what the snake had said.

Amy thought, "Let's see. Are they right in what they're saying? I don't think so. I don't think my skin is too saggy for a hippopotamus."

So Amy didn't give another thought to what they had said.

Amy's husband Ralph was by the pond. When Ralph saw Amy, he said to her, "Amy, you're about the prettiest thing I ever laid eyes on."

Amy thought to herself, "Let's see; I do feel good about that! I do care about what Ralph thinks."

Amy said, "Thanks, Ralph. You're pretty handsome, big boy." And she gave him a kiss on the cheek.

Alex Lets Jimmy Sit on the Bicycle

Alex was riding his bicycle. Jimmy, a boy Alex knew, ran up to Alex.

Jimmy said, "Hey Alex, let me ride your bicycle, please!"

Alex thought, "What should I do? If I let him try to ride, his legs won't reach the pedals. He'll fall over."

Illustrated Stories That Model Psychological Skills

Then Alex thought, "I could just say, 'No.' to Jimmy. That would be better than his hurting himself, but he'd be disappointed."

Then Alex thought, "I know what I can do! I can lift him up on my bicycle and hold him while he sits there for a minute or two."

So Alex said, "Jimmy, your legs are too short to ride the bike, but I'll let you sit on the seat."

Alex let Jimmy sit on the bike seat. Alex was very careful not to let Jimmy fall. Jimmy had fun.

Alex Lets Jimmy Sit on the Bicycle

Jimmy said, "Thanks, Alex!" Alex said, "You're welcome, Jimmy." Alex felt good because he had made a good decision and had let Jimmy have a good time.

Rusty Helps Tommy Learn to Swim 	One time, Rusty was at a swimming pool. 
People were trying to get Tommy to go into the pool, but Tommy wouldn't do it. Tommy was scared. 	Rusty said to Tommy, "What's the matter, Tommy? Can I help you?" 

Rusty Helps Tommy Learn To Swim

Tommy said, "I can't swim. That's why I don't want to go in."
Rusty said, "Would you like a little swimming lesson from me?"

Tommy said, "Yes, Rusty, I'd like that." So first they just dangled their feet in the shallow water.

Then Rusty showed Tommy how to hold his breath and put his face under water.

Then Rusty showed Tommy how to float face down in the water.

Tommy did as Rusty had showed him. Rusty said, "That's good, Tommy!"

Then Rusty showed Tommy how to move his arms when he swam.

Tommy did what Rusty had done. Rusty said, "Good for you, Tommy!"

Then Rusty showed Tommy how to kick with his legs. When Tommy did it, Rusty said, "I'm proud of you, Tommy!"

Rusty Helps Tommy Learn To Swim

Then, Rusty said, "Here's how you put it all together."

Tommy did it like Rusty had done. Rusty said, "Hooray for you, Tommy!"

Rusty said, "You did it! You swam some!" Tommy felt good.

Rusty felt good that he had been able to help Tommy.

Illustrated Stories That Model Psychological Skills

Margo Feeds the Birds

It was a very cold winter. Margo saw the birds out in the cold.

The birds could not get enough food to eat. All of them were very cold and hungry and some of them were even starving to death.

Margo thought, "I want to feed the birds."

Margo Feeds the Birds

Margo got some of the money that she had saved up. 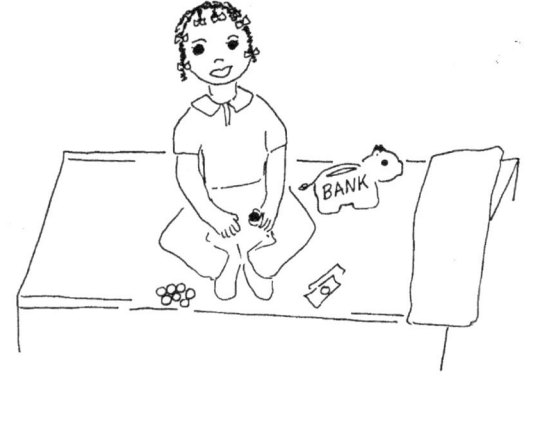	Margo went to the store and bought some seeds for the birds. 
Margo put the seeds out for the birds. 	At first the birds wouldn't come to the food that Margo had left for them. 

Finally they came and ate the birdseed. Margo felt really good that she was able to help them.

Margo kept feeding them throughout the rest of the winter. She watched them from her bedroom window.

Charlie Helps His Brother

Charlie Helps His Brother

One time there was a boy named Charlie who had a younger brother named Ted. One day they decided to go out and throw a baseball.

Charlie knew that Ted was working hard at learning to catch fly balls. So Charlie would throw the ball way up into the air for Ted to catch.

But Ted missed three or four in a row. Ted felt mad at himself for missing the balls so much.

Illustrated Stories That Model Psychological Skills

Ted said, "Why do I keep missing! What's the matter with me?"

Charlie went up to Ted and put his arm around Ted's shoulder. Charlie said, "I can help you out, Ted."

Charlie said, "Don't be so hard on yourself when you miss a ball. Just take it easy."

Charlie said, "I think you'll catch more if you relax. But even if you miss every single one, it's OK anyway."

Charlie Helps His Brother

After that, Ted did take it easier and he started catching the balls.

When he would miss, he would smile at Charlie and Charlie would smile back. And he wouldn't let himself get bothered.

They had a good time together. Charlie felt good that he had been able to help his brother.

Illustrated Stories That Model Psychological Skills

Louis Fastens the Seat Belt

Louis's mother said, "Let's go to get some food!"

Louis and his friend Mario said, "Okay, we'll go with you."

Louis's mother said, "You boys remember to put your seat belts on."

Louis Fastens the Seat Belt

Louis said to Mario, "Yes, let's put our seat belts on."

So Louis and Mario both put on their seat belts.

As they were driving, another car ran a red light.

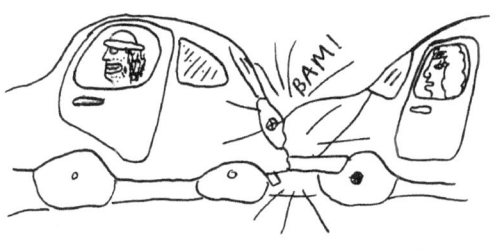

Louis's mother's car wrecked into the other car.

Illustrated Stories That Model Psychological Skills

Louis and Mario would have smashed into the front of the car, but their seat belts had held them safely.

Louis's mother said, "Are you boys all right?"

Louis and Mario said, "Yes, we weren't hurt at all. Are you OK?" Louis's mother and the other driver weren't hurt either. They had all been saved by seat belts.

Louis's mother said, "I'm sorry we had a wreck, but I'm really happy that you did what I asked you to and put your seat belts on." Louis felt good that he had done that too.

The Witch and the Wizard Talk Out Their Problem

The Witch and the Wizard Talk Out Their Problem

One day an owl flew by, and one of his feathers fell off. A witch and a wizard saw what happened.

The witch said, "Oh, this is good! I needed an owl's feather for my brew. I'll mix it with bat's teeth and frogs' spit."

The wizard said, "So, you need the feather! I need it too, for my potion. If I mix it with lizard tears and mice's toenails, I can do all sorts of magic things!"

Illustrated Stories That Model Psychological Skills

The witch said, "Let's see. What can we do? We can flip a coin and let the person who wins take the feather." The wizard said, "Or, we could let one of us use it this time and the other of us use it the next time. We could take turns.

The witch said, "I know! Since we each need only a little bit of feather, we could cut it in half. Each of us can take half."
The wizard said, "That's a good idea; I like that one best."

So, they cut the feather in two so that they could each have some of it.

So they each were able to make their magic potions.

The Witch and the Wizard Talk Out Their Problem

And they were each able to do magic things with their magic potions.

And they all had a good time.

Illustrated Stories That Model Psychological Skills

Hank Doesn't Get to Go to the Zoo

One morning, Hank got dressed in a hurry. He was excited. His uncle was going to take him to the zoo.

He waited for his Uncle to come. He thought about the animals he was going to see.

All of a sudden the phone rang. Hank's mother answered it.

Hank Doesn't Get to Go to the Zoo

Hank's mother said, "This is your uncle. Something came up and he can't take you to the zoo today."

After Hank had talked to his uncle, he thought to himself, "Let's see, what can I do now? I can mope around and be sad, or throw a tantrum and get mad, if I want to."

Hank thought to himself, "Or I could try to go to the zoo by myself on a bus. Or, I could try to get some of my friends to play soccer with me."

Hank decided to get his friends to play soccer with him. He called them on the phone and said, "Do you want to play soccer?"

Illustrated Stories That Model Psychological Skills

Hank was able to get some friends together to play soccer. They had a fun game. Hank made a goal.

Later that evening, Hank's uncle came over. Hank heard him talk to his mother. Hank's uncle said, "I'm sorry I couldn't take Hank to the zoo. Was he very upset?"

Hank's mother said, "He was disappointed, but he took it really well. He found something else to do very fast. He really knows how to take it when things don't go his way." Hank knew this was true, and he felt proud of himself.

Kenny and Jerry and the Alligators

Kenny and Jerry and the Alligators

Jerry was walking outside. He was so young that he didn't know how to read.

Jerry opened a gate and went inside a fence.

Kenny saw what happened.

Illustrated Stories That Model Psychological Skills

Kenny was old enough to read the sign. The sign said, "Watch out for alligators."

Kenny went to Jerry and said, "Jerry, we need to leave now." And Jerry did what Kenny asked him to do.

Kenny said, "The reason we need to leave is that the sign said there might be alligators in here. It was good of you to come with me when I asked you to."

Jerry said, "What's an alligator, Kenny?".

Kenny and Jerry and the Alligators

Kenny said, "An alligator is a big, green animal that crawls or swims that has a great big mouth with lots of sharp teeth."

Jerry said, "Oh, so an alligator is like those animals there."

Jerry said, "You know, they look like they could eat us up. I'm glad you came with me when you asked me to, Kenny. Thanks for taking me out of there."

Kenny felt good that he had saved Jerry from the alligators.

Jan Tells Her Brother a Story

Jan had a younger brother named Mike. Mike was watching a scary TV show.

That night when it was time for Mike to go to bed, Mike was scared. Mike came to Jan and said, "May I stay in your room? I'm scared."

Jan said, "I'll sit in your room with you, Mike. I'll tell you a story."

Jan Tells Her Brother a Story

Jan sat by Mike's bed. She started to tell her story.

Here is the story Jan told.
Once upon a time there was a little boy named Wolfie. He was sitting down crying.

Mike came up to Wolfie. He said, "What's the matter? Can I help you?"
Wolfie said, "I'm crying because people don't like me."

Then Wolfie said, "They don't like me because I've got hair all over my face and my teeth are too long and crooked." And Wolfie showed his face to Mike and his face did look really unusual. But Mike was not scared.

Jan Tells Her Brother a Story

Mike said, "I don't care what you look like. Come and play with me."

Mike took Wolfie home and gave him some pudding with a great big cherry on it.

Then Mike threw a football with Wolfie.

Mike introduced Wolfie to his friends. When they got to know him, they started to like him too.

Jan Tells Her Brother a Story

Wolfie did lots of nice things for Mike. Wolfie showed Mike some nice places he'd found in the woods. Mike was glad he'd become friends with Wolfie.

That was the end of Jan's story. Jan could see that Mike looked very peaceful and relaxed.

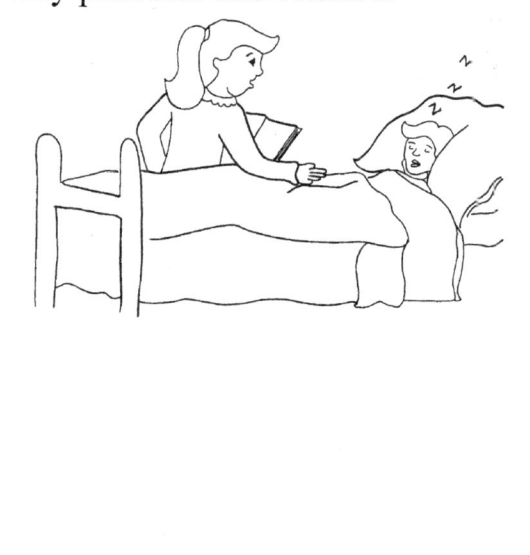

Jan felt good that she had helped her brother not to be scared.

Illustrated Stories That Model Psychological Skills

Linda Takes Care of Her Baby Doll

Linda said to her mother, "Mother, will you read me a story?"

Linda's mother said, "I can't now, Linda. I'm putting the baby to bed."

At first, Linda felt mad.

Linda Takes Care of Her Baby Doll

But then she got an idea. She said to herself, "I'll put *my* baby doll to bed."

Linda brought her doll into the bedroom where her mother was. Linda said, "I'm putting my doll to bed, too."
Linda's mother said, "That's a great idea."

Linda's mother said, "I'm going to rock the baby in my arms some. Do you want to rock your baby?"

Linda said, "Yes, I'll rock my baby too."

Illustrated Stories That Model Psychological Skills

Then Linda's mother and Linda both put their babies to bed.

Someone rang the doorbell. Linda let the person in. It was one of her mother's friends.

The friend looked at Linda's mother's baby. Linda's mother said, "Look at Linda's baby. She's sleeping too."

The friend looked at the doll and said, "My, what a pretty baby. I'll bet Linda takes good care of it."

Linda Takes Care of Her Baby Doll

Linda felt happy.

Jason Tames the Horse

There was a horse named Tornado. The men decided to try to ride him for the first time.

When the first man got on Tornado's back, Tornado bucked him off.

More men tried to ride Tornado, but Tornado bucked them all off.

Jason Tames the Horse

A boy named Jason said to them, "I bet I can tame him." But the men just laughed at him.

Jason started being very nice to Tornado. He fed him and gave him water.

Jason brushed Tornado's hide in a way that felt really good for Tornado.

Little by little, Tornado came to trust Jason. Tornado would let Jason pet him.

Illustrated Stories That Model Psychological Skills

Then one day Jason lay over Tornado's back.

And then Jason actually sat on Tornado's back.

A few days later, the men saw Jason riding Tornado. They were very surprised. They said, "How did you ever do that?"

Jason said, "I was just nice to him and let him learn to trust me."

Maurice Shows a Book to a New Boy

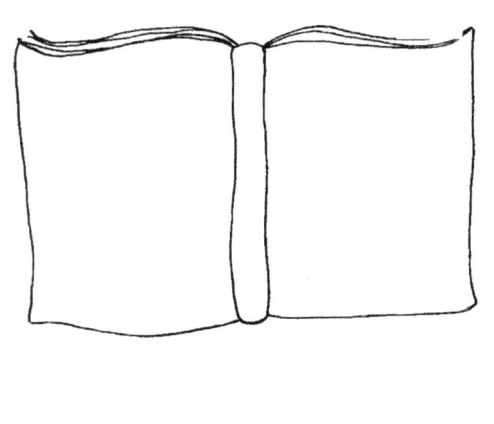

One day John's mother said, "We're going someplace new today. It's a preschool."

When they got to the new place, there were lots of children. John didn't know any of them.

John's mother said, "Bye-bye, John. I'll see you in a few hours."

Maurice Shows a Book to a New Boy

Maurice saw what happened. He saw John looking upset. Maurice said to himself, "I want to help him."

Maurice got a book. He came up to John and said, "Would you like to look at this book with me?"

Maurice showed the book to John. Maurice could tell that John was feeling better now.

The teacher said, "Hey, Maurice and John. I like the way you are playing together. Do you like that book?"

John said, "Yes, I like this book a lot." Maurice felt good that he had helped John feel better.

Jean Comforts Her Baby Sister

Jean Comforts Her Baby Sister

Jean had a baby sister. The baby was asleep.

Jean's baby sister woke up crying. Jean thought, "She wants someone to be with her."

Jean went to tell her mother. But her mother was busy.

Illustrated Stories That Model Psychological Skills

Jean thought to herself, "I'll go to my baby sister myself." So that's what she did.

Jean touched her baby sister very gently.

Jean talked very softly to the baby. She said, "You just wanted somebody to be with you, didn't you? You were lonesome."

Jean held a toy where the baby could see it. Jean enjoyed watching the baby reach for it and look at it.

Jean Comforts Her Baby Sister

Soon the baby went back to sleep.

Jean's mother was still too busy to notice what had happened. But Jean felt good that she had been able to make her sister feel better and to help her mother.

The Boy and the Video Machines

Once a boy was in a shopping mall with his mother.

He saw a store that looked very interesting. It had video games that you could try out for free.

The boy said to his mother, "I would like to go and look around in that store!"

The Boy and the Video Machines

But his mother said, "We can't do that now. I need to get home right now, because I am in a hurry."

The boy had the urge to nag and gripe and complain and keep begging his mother. He also had the urge just to run to the store and take a quick look.

But he said to himself, "I guess I can put up with not being able to see it for now."

He walked along with his mother and said to her, "The next time we are here, maybe I can go look around in that store while you are in the other stores. Then we can meet someplace afterward."

Illustrated Stories That Model Psychological Skills

His mother answered, "I think that sounds like a good idea."

The next time they went to the mall, that is just what they did.

His mother said to him afterward, "You were able to do this because you showed so much self-control the last time. You could leave when you didn't feel like it."

The boy was very glad that things had worked out the way they had.

Michael Gives Back the Magic Wand

Michael Gives Back the Magic Wand

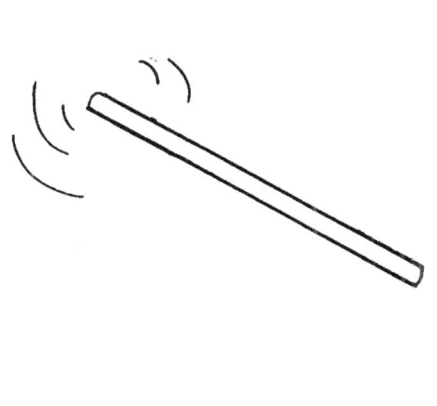

One day Michael found a stick on the ground.

Michael soon found out that the stick was a magic wand! He could turn an apple…

…into an apple pie.

Then he turned an old beat-up tire...

...into a shiny new car.

Michael was thrilled about having a magic wand. But the next morning, a wizard came to his door. The wizard said, "I've lost a magic wand. Have you seen it anywhere?"

Michael didn't want to give up the magic wand. But he was always honest. And he somehow knew that the wizard was the rightful owner of the wand. So he gave the wand back.

Michael Gives Back the Magic Wand

The wizard said, "Thanks, Michael. You were very honest and you helped me a lot!" Michael felt good that he had done the right thing.

The next morning, when Michael woke up, he found by his pillow a book. There was a note in the book that said, "Dear Michael, this is a magic book for you. You can look up in it the answer to any question you have. Thanks again for returning my wand. Your friend, The Wizard."

At first, Michael wasn't excited about having the book. But then he began to find out how useful it was. One day a pipe broke in Michael's apartment, and water was going all over everywhere.

The book told Michael just how to fix the pipe.

Illustrated Stories That Model Psychological Skills

Another time, Michael's dog got hit by a car.

The book told Michael just what to do. Michael was able to save his dog's life.

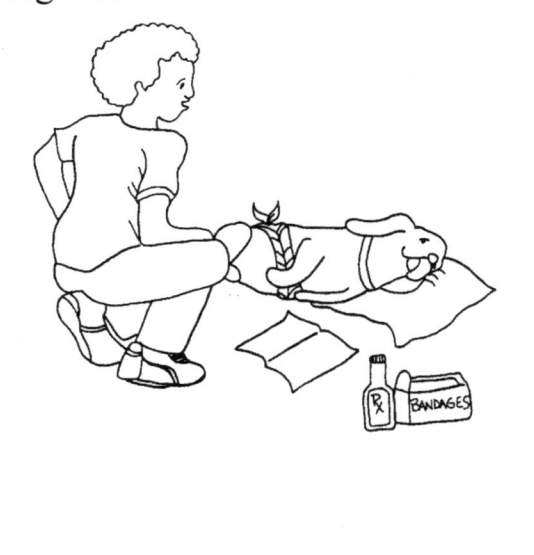

Michael wrote a thank you letter to the wizard. He said, "Dear Mr. Wizard, thank you for the book. So far I've used it to fix a pipe and to save my dog's life. I hope things are going well for you. Your friend, Michael"

Larry and the Monkey

Larry and the Monkey

Larry liked to help his father.

His father worked at a zoo. One day, Larry was helping his father clean up near the monkeys.

Larry thought it was really amazing that they could jump and climb and hang by their tails.

He got the urge to stick his hand through the bars and into the monkey area. He felt like trying to touch a monkey.

But, then he said to himself, "Wait a minute. Let me think about this… They look very cute, but…"

"…they still might bite my finger. I think I won't stick my finger in there."

While he was thinking about this, Larry stuck a little stick just a little bit through the bars.

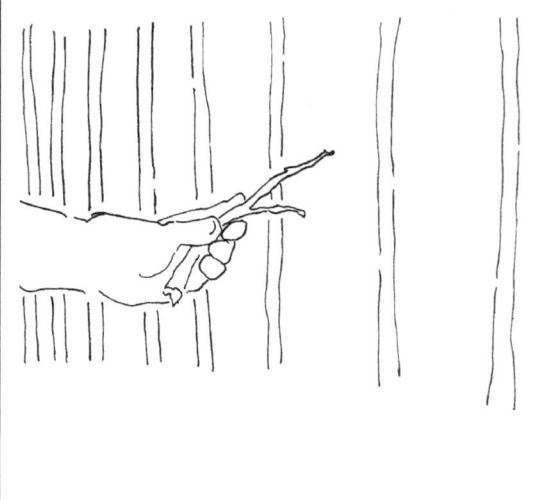

Larry and the Monkey

Sure enough, one of the monkeys came up and bit the stick without even taking time to look at what it was.

The monkey bit hard! He bit the end of the stick off.

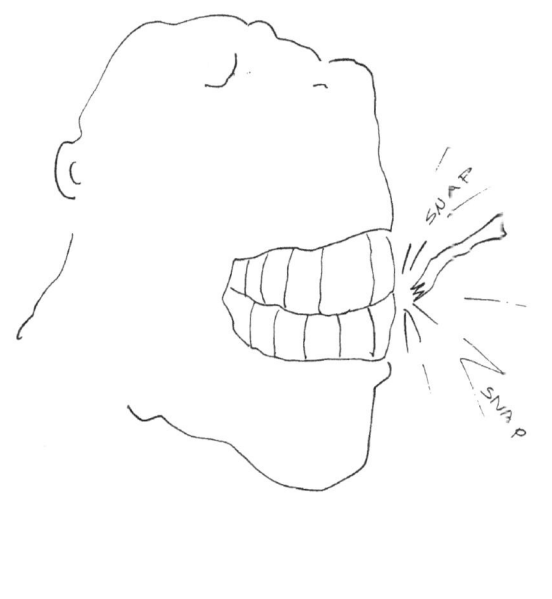

Larry thought to himself, "I'm glad I thought before I acted. Otherwise, it might have been the end of my finger that the monkey bit off!"

Larry enjoyed watching the monkeys many times after that.

The Man and the Lion

Once a man was walking on a long trip through the woods. All of a sudden he heard a loud roaring noise.

He saw all sorts of animals running away. They were afraid of what was roaring.

But this man went toward the roaring to see what it was.

The Man and the Lion

The sound was coming from a big lion who was lying down and groaning. Most people would have been afraid, but this man was not. He loved animals and knew them very well.

The man also had very sharp eyes. He could see that the lion was roaring because he had a thorn in his paw.

The man thought, "That thorn probably hurts the lion badly. This may be foolish, but I'm going to help him."

The man went up and took the thorn out of the lion's paw. The lion was so grateful that he licked the man on the face, just as a dog does sometimes.

Illustrated Stories That Model Psychological Skills

The man felt very good that he had been able to help the lion. He went along on his journey. 	A long time after that, a bad king captured the man and planned to kill him. 
The king and a lot of other people took the man out and put him in a big pen. Then they let a big lion loose in the pen. 	They thought that the lion would eat the man. But a strange look came upon the lion's face. The lion remembered the man. It was the same lion that the man had helped! 

The Man and the Lion

The lion licked the man on the face, just as he had before. And then the lion took the man on his back.

The lion jumped over the wall of the pen. They both got away from the king and his people. They lived happily from then on.

Illustrated Stories That Model Psychological Skills

Mr. Monster Helps Mrs. Monster 	A couple of slimy monsters lived in a cave. 
There was a husband monster and a wife monster. 	They were not like people, who like nice warm, dry beds at night. Instead, they could only sleep well if they slept on cold, wet slime. 

Mr. Monster Helps Mrs. Monster

One night, Mr. Monster and Mrs. Monster were sleeping. Mrs. Monster was not sleeping well.

She was tossing and turning and acting very restless.

Mr. Monster figured out what the problem was. There was not enough slime on her side of their bed.

So he got up and got some more slime and put it on her side of the bed.

Pretty soon she gave a big smile. She settled down and slept very soundly.	She didn't wake up the whole time that he did this. Still, he felt really good that he had helped her sleep better and feel more rested in the morning.

Lucia Helps Her Mother Change the Baby's Diapers

Lucia Helps Her Mother Change the Baby's Diapers

Lucia wanted her mother to be with her.

When Lucia found her mother, her mother was getting ready to change the baby's diapers. At first Lucia felt sad, because she wanted her mother to herself.

But then Lucia had an idea. She said, "Mother, may I help you change the baby's diaper?"

Illustrated Stories That Model Psychological Skills

Lucia's mother said, "Hey, thanks for offering to help, Lucia! Yes, there are some things you can do. Can you fill up this bowl with warm water and bring it back to me?"

Lucia brought the water. Lucia's mother said, "What a good helper you are! Now I'll wipe off the baby with a washrag and the water you brought me. Can you now bring me the bag so I can put this dirty diaper in it?"

Lucia brought the bag and they put the dirty diaper in it. Lucia's mother said, "Thank you, Lucia, you're a big help."

Then Lucia's mother showed Lucia how to fold the diaper and put it on the baby.

Lucia Helps Her Mother Change the Baby's Diapers

Later on, Lucia's father came home. Lucia's mother said, "Guess what Lucia did? She helped me change the baby's diaper!"

Lucia's father said, "Good for you, Lucia! You're a good helper." Lucia felt good.

Illustrated Stories That Model Psychological Skills

Helen and Her Brother

Once there was a girl named Helen.

She had a little brother named Jerry.

One night their parents were going to be out late. They got a babysitter to stay with Helen and Jerry.

Helen and Her Brother

But their regular babysitter couldn't come. The woman who came was stern looking and didn't smile.

Helen didn't particularly care, but she could see that Jerry looked nervous and sad. He missed his parents. So, Helen said to herself, "I'll see if I can take care of Jerry so he'll feel better."

When it was close to Jerry's bedtime, Helen said, "Jerry, why don't you get your pajamas on and get in bed, and I'll read you a story."

Jerry did get ready for bed. Helen picked out a good story to read to him that wasn't very scary.

Then she turned the lights out and stayed in his room with him singing him songs.

After a while, she noticed that he looked very peaceful and relaxed.

Helen said good night and left his room. She said to herself, "I think I made him feel very safe and protected." She felt good that she had been able to be kind to him.

Brian Sees the Glove

Brian Sees the Glove

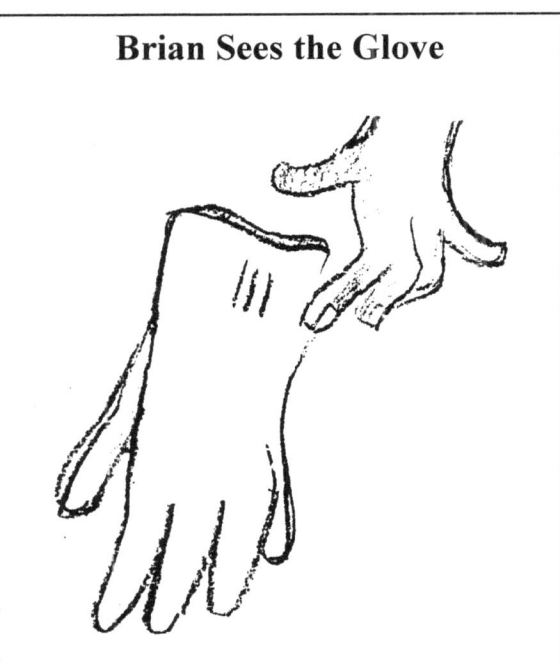

Once Brian was out taking a walk.

Brian saw a woman getting out of her car. This woman looked tense and scared. Brian wondered if she were afraid someone would attack her.

As she walked down the sidewalk, she dropped her glove, without noticing that she had dropped it.

Illustrated Stories That Model Psychological Skills

Brian said, "Excuse me, Ma'am, you dropped your glove."

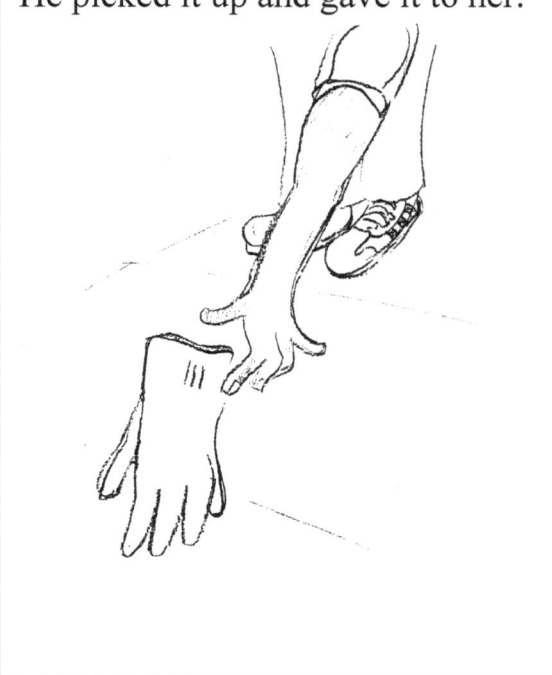
He picked it up and gave it to her.

The woman smiled and thanked Brian and then walked away.

But as she walked, she didn't look nearly so scared and tense as she had before.

Brian felt good. He thought, "I not only helped her not to lose her glove; I also made her feel less scared."

Illustrated Stories That Model Psychological Skills

Teddy and His Resting Mother

Teddy was at home.

He had just gotten a new book. He really wanted his mother to read him a story. He could hardly wait to hear the stories in it.

He took his book and ran through the house looking for his mother.

Teddy and His Resting Mother

When he found her, she was lying on the couch with her eyes closed. He got the urge to yell, "Mommy, can you read to me please?"

But then he thought to himself, "She's tired, and she needs to rest now. I'll wait until later when she's through resting."

So, he waited. He felt good, because he knew he was helping her and making her feel better.

Rusty Helps Timmy Fetch His Dog

Rusty Helps Timmy Fetch His Dog

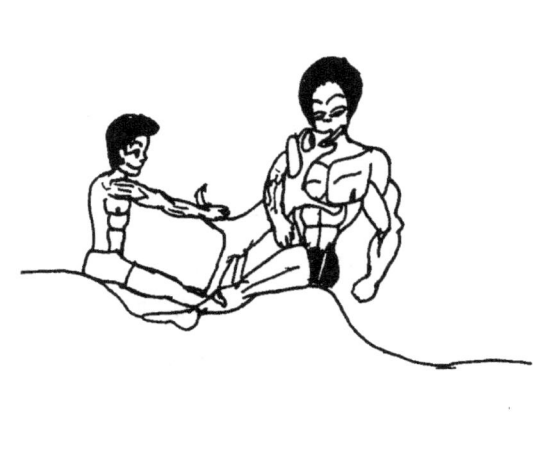

Timmy and his dog Frederick were at the beach.

It became time for Timmy to take Frederick home. Timmy called, "Here, Frederick."

But Frederick would not come.

Rusty Helps Timmy Fetch His Dog

Timmy ran after Frederick, but that only scared Frederick. Frederick ran away.

Timmy was so mad that he got the urge to throw sand at Frederick. He didn't do it; he just felt like it. But just then Rusty came up to Timmy.

Rusty said, "Timmy, I'll help you fetch your dog."

Rusty said, "Let's sit down. Be nice to him and he'll come to us. If you yell at him and run after him, you only scare him away."

Rusty Helps Timmy Fetch His Dog

Pretty soon, Frederick came up to them, just as Rusty had said he would.

They had a good time petting Frederick.

Timmy said, "Thanks, Rusty. You helped us both out."

Lester Helps the Jumping Elf

Lester Helps the Jumping Elf

Once there were some jumping elves. Their legs were so strong that they could jump very far. They could jump to the tops of mountains.

If they came to the city, they could easily jump to the top of the highest buildings.

One of the jumping elves hurt his leg. He couldn't jump back home, and so he was stuck in the city.

Illustrated Stories That Model Psychological Skills

Most of the children laughed at him because he looked different.

But Lester felt sorry for the jumping elf. He said, "Are you hurt? Would you like some help?"

Lester took the jumping elf to his house. He let him sleep there and gave him food while his leg was healing.

Lester read stories to the jumping elf to keep him from getting bored.

Lester Helps the Jumping Elf

Finally the jumping elf got well. The jumping elf said, "Lester, you've been really nice to me. I want to do something nice for you. Climb onto my back."

So Lester got onto the jumping-elf's back and they jumped way up into the sky.

They landed on a high mountain. The jumping elf said, "Now you get a special treat, Lester. We're going to the moon."

Lester enjoyed the trip through space.

Illustrated Stories That Model Psychological Skills

It was great fun to be on the moon and to look down at Earth.

Then they jumped back toward Earth and Lester's home.

Lester said, "Thank you for that wonderful trip, Mr. Jumping Elf!" And the jumping elf said, "Thank you for helping me, Lester, when no one else would help me."

Lester said good-bye to his friend.

Maggie and Mrs. Robinson

Maggie and Mrs. Robinson

Some children had lunch every day at their school cafeteria.

One of the ladies that gave them their food looked very crabby and unhappy. Some of the children stuck their tongues out at her as they went through the line.

But Maggie noticed that the woman looked sad. Maggie thought, "I'll try to cheer her up."

Illustrated Stories That Model Psychological Skills

So, one day as she went through the line, she looked at the lady, and the lady looked at her.

Maggie smiled and said, "Hi. I hope you're having a good day."

The woman looked up, surprised, and said, "Why, thank you!"

The next day, Maggie said to the woman, "Hello again, today. What's your name?"

Maggie and Mrs. Robinson

And the lady said, "My name's Mrs. Robinson. What's yours?" And Maggie said, "My name's Maggie."

And then every day after that, Maggie would speak to Mrs. Robinson. One day she said, "How are you doing today, Mrs. Robinson?" One day she said, "That's a pretty scarf, Mrs. Robinson."

Pretty soon some of the other children who saw Maggie started doing this too. Mrs. Robinson started smiling and being nice to the children. She started looking happy.

From then on, when Maggie went through the line, she felt good, because she knew that she had helped Mrs. Robinson to enjoy her job.

Joe and Larry Get the Tree

Once there was a boy named Joe. He lived on a big farm with lots of woods. Joe's family wanted to use a tree for a holiday celebration. After that, they would use the wood to make things. Joe was old enough to go out into the woods and chop down a tree for his family.

It was a snowy and cold day. He took his ax and started to leave the house. Just then his little brother Larry said, "Hey Joe, may I come with you?"

Joe said, "Sure, but it's a long way to the woods and it's cold out, so be sure to put lots of clothes on." So Larry put on lots of sweaters and a coat and the two of them left together.

Joe and Larry Get the Tree

They walked for a long way. Joe said, "Are you cold?"

Larry said, "Most of me is warm, but my toes are freezing."

By this time Joe had picked out a tree and in only a few minutes had chopped it down. Then he said to Larry, "Larry, I've got an idea. Take your shoes off. I'll put you on my shoulders and you can slip your feet down inside my coat. Your feet can warm themselves up by resting against me."

Larry did what Joe told him to. Soon Joe was walking home carrying the ax in one hand, the tree in the other and Larry on his shoulders. Larry's feet rested right against Joe's sides.

At first the feet were cold. Joe said, "You weren't kidding. Those feet are cold! But they'll warm up. I'll bet your hands are cold too. Put them on me and they'll warm up also. There, how's that?"

Larry said, "My hands and feet are warm now. Thanks a lot, Joe."

When they got home, Larry told his mother and father what Joe had done. Their father smiled at Joe and said, "That must have been a heavy load, Joe."

And Joe said, "That's right. That Larry is getting so big, I won't be able to carry him much longer." Joe felt good that he and Larry had had a good time together.

James Lind Does An Experiment

James Lind Does An Experiment

One time there was a very bad disease called scurvy. Sailors often got it when they were in ocean ships for a long time.

People with scurvy would have their gums swell and get very sore. They would get purple bruises all over their bodies.

They would feel weak and tired. Their legs would swell. Old scars would open and bleed. Very many people died of this disease.

No one knew what caused it or how to get it better. In the year 1747 a man named James Lind was on a ship. His job was to take care of the sick men.

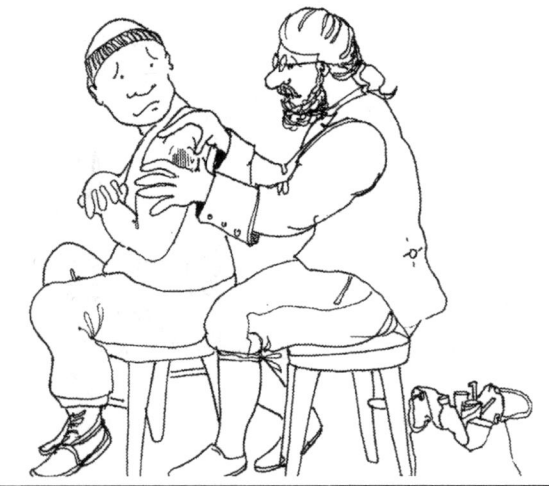

James Lind read about different things that other people thought might help people with scurvy. Some people thought that vinegar would help. Some people said to drink sea water.

Some people thought that the best thing was a paste mixed up from all sorts of other stuff. Someone else claimed that lemons and limes and oranges would be best.

James Lind got the idea to do an experiment. In an experiment, you try out things and see what happens. He first made sure that the men in his experiment got the same thing to eat each day.

James Lind Does An Experiment

Then he gave vinegar to some of them and salt water to some of them.

He gave the paste to some of them and he gave oranges and lemons to some of them. He tried other things with still others of them.

For two weeks, each man got the same treatment each day. Lind wrote down each day how each of them was doing.

At the end of the two weeks, the men who had gotten the sea water and the ones who had gotten the vinegar and the ones who had gotten the paste were still just as sick as they had been.

But the ones who had gotten the oranges and lemons had gotten well! They felt so good that they could get up and work and try to help the other men.

James Lind wrote down what had happened in his experiment, so that other people could know about it. He wrote down that oranges and lemons were the best way to get people better when they have scurvy.

It took a long time before people paid attention to what he had written. When they did, they started taking lots of lemons and limes and oranges whenever they went on a long trip on the sea. They made sure that all the sailors ate one of these each day.

When they did this, the men didn't get scurvy any more.

James Lind Does An Experiment

We still remember James Lind, even though it is now more than 300 years since he did his experiment. People have now discovered that the stuff in lemons and oranges that kept people from getting scurvy is something we call Vitamin C.

James Lind's experiments helped a lot of people not to get scurvy. It also showed doctors how to do experiments to see what works the best for other diseases. It did a lot of good for a lot of people.

Jack Saves the Man From Freezing

It was winter in the North Woods. Jack was staying with his friends in a cabin. He got lots of wood for his fire.

Not very far off, a man was going through the North Woods on a dog sled.

The man stopped so that he and the dogs could rest. He let the dogs run loose.

Jack Saves the Man from Freezing

All of a sudden a rabbit started running away, and the dogs started chasing it.

The man made a mistake. He went running after the dogs. If he had stayed where he was, the dogs would have come back after a while.

The man ran around looking for the dogs for a long time. Meanwhile, it began to snow very hard. The man realized that he was lost in the woods.

It began to get very cold. The man had two matches. He tried to build a fire. But he made another mistake. He used wet wood.

Both matches went out. The man was very cold. He thought to himself, "Maybe I'll freeze to death out here."

He looked for his sled as long as he could. Then he fell on the snow, because he was too tired to try anymore.

He went to sleep. After a while, his dogs found him. They sat and howled very loudly, but he did not wake up.

Jack was at his cabin. He heard the howling dogs. He said to himself, "I wonder if someone needs help." He decided he would go and look.

Jack Saves the Man from Freezing

Jack used a map and a compass to keep track of where he was in the woods. He said to himself, "It's easy to get lost in these woods. I'll not get lost, though." He went toward where he heard the sound.

Finally Jack found the man and the dogs. The snow had almost covered the man up. Jack said to himself, "I wonder if he's frozen to death."

Jack saw that the man was still alive. Jack said to himself, "I'll put my coat on him; I'll keep myself warm from the exercise I'm going to get."

Jack picked up the man and carried him back toward his cabin. Jack said to himself, "He's heavy, but I think I can carry him anyway." The dogs came along.

They finally got back to the cabin. Jack said to himself, "Hooray, I made it."

Jack took the man inside and put him in a warm bed. He built the fire up and made some hot cocoa for the man.

The man drank the hot cocoa. The man said, "Thank you. You saved my life. I would have frozen to death if it hadn't been for you."

Jack and his friends decided they could trust the man to stay with them. Jack said, "Tomorrow we'll go and find your sled. I feel good that we're able to help you."

Ralph Helps the People Keep Warm

Ralph's house was right in front of a bus stop. One day, it was very cold outside. The wind was blowing hard.

Even if people had lots of winter clothes on, the wind blew against their faces and stung them. Most people tried to stay inside on that day.

Ralph was looking out his front window and he saw a woman and two children waiting outside for the bus. They looked very cold and were huddled together trying to keep warm.

As Ralph thought about the cold outside, he felt sorry for them and felt a wish to take care of them. He ran to his mother and said, "Mother, there are a woman and two children outside waiting for the bus in the cold. May I invite them inside to wait in here until the bus comes?"

His mother said, "Hmm. That sounds like a nice idea. Let me take a look." His mother looked from the front door and said, "I know who those people are. Yes, why don't you invite them in? We can watch for the bus from the front window."

So Ralph put on his coat and went outside. He said to them, "Hi! It's cold today, isn't it? You're waiting for the bus, aren't you?"

Ralph said, "How would you like to come inside our house to wait? You can watch from the front window."

The woman looked at her children and saw how cold they were and she said, "I appreciate this, very much."

As they walked inside, Ralph's mother said to them, "Welcome. Please come in and get out of those bitter cold winds."

While they were waiting, Ralph stood and talked with them. His mother brought them all some hot chocolate. She said, "I put these in the type of cups that you can throw away, so that you can take them with you if the bus comes."

After a while, Ralph saw the bus coming. So he ran out to make sure the driver would stop. The woman and the children said, "Thank you, Ralph," as they got on the bus.

The woman carried an extra cup in her hand with a lid on the top. When Ralph got back inside, he asked his mother what the extra cup was for. She said, "That was for the bus driver. He can drink it during that long stop a few blocks up the street."

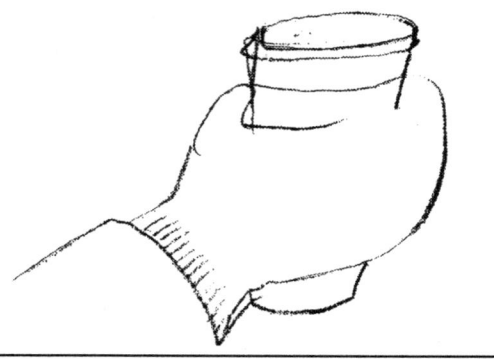

Paul Reads to His Mother

Paul Reads to His Mother

Paul wanted his mother to go outside with him and take a walk.

Paul said, "Mother, would you like to take a walk with me?"
She said, "I can't now, Paul. I'm feeding the baby."

Paul thought, "Let's see, what could I do now? I could take a walk by myself."

Illustrated Stories That Model Psychological Skills

Paul thought, "Or I could read a book by myself."

Paul thought, "Or, I could see if my mother would like to hear me read a book to her while she feeds the baby. I think I like that idea the best."

Paul found a good book. He said, "Mother, how would you like to hear this book while you feed the baby?"

Paul's mother said, "Yes, I'd like that very much, Paul." So, Paul started to read the story to his mother.

Paul Reads to His Mother

As Paul read, Paul's mother said to the baby, "Isn't this a good story! I'm so glad you have a big brother who knows how to read! This makes my job lots more fun."

Paul felt good that he was helping his mother have a good time.

Illustrated Stories That Model Psychological Skills

Gina Forgives Her Brother

One day, Gina's mother gave Gina a little doll made of china.

This doll was very easy to break, but Gina loved it and took very good care of it.

One day Gina left the doll on the table for just a little while. Gina's brother Ralph saw the doll. Ralph was almost two years old.

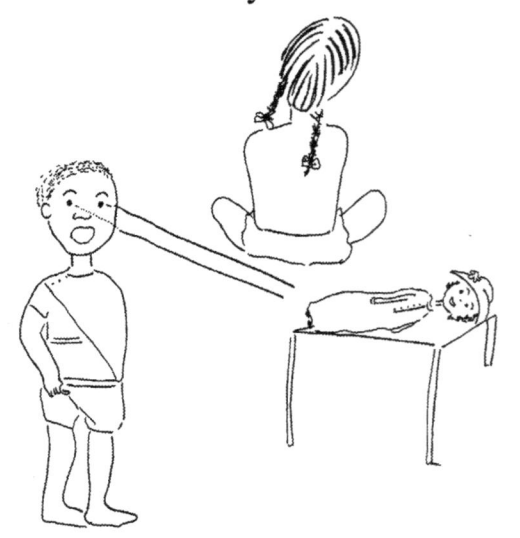

Gina Forgives Her Brother

Ralph climbed up and reached for the doll. But he knocked it off and broke it into a thousand pieces.

Gina was upset when she saw that her favorite doll was broken. She also felt mad at her brother.

But then Gina said, "I forgive you, Ralph, because you didn't know what you were doing. Come on, I'll move you away from those broken pieces of china so you won't cut yourself. Then I'll just sweep up the pieces."

Gina's mother said, "You did something really good, Gina."

Gina's mother said, "Your doll was something nice, but your kindness to your brother was even nicer." Gina felt good.

Mack Helps the Little Girl

Mack Helps the Little Girl

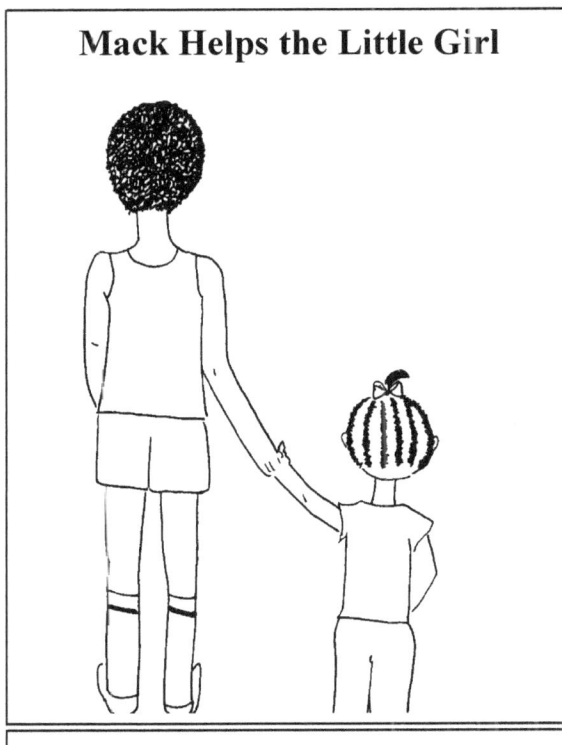

Once Mack was in a grocery store.

A little girl a lot younger than Mack came up to him.

She looked like she was about to cry. Mack said, "What's the matter; can I help you?"

Illustrated Stories That Model Psychological Skills

The little girl said, "I can't find my mother."
Mack took her by the hand and said, "Don't worry, we'll find her."

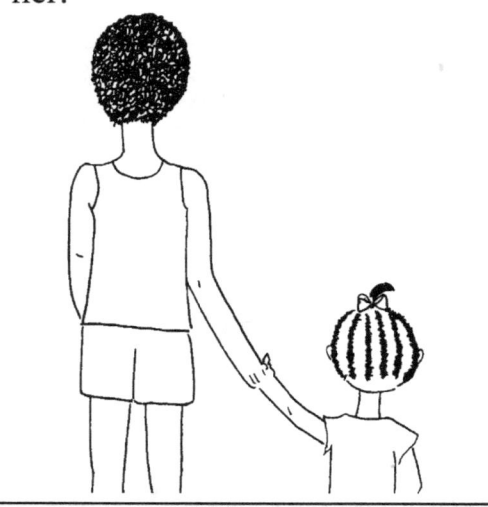

Mack took the little girl to the back of the store where they could look down the first aisle.

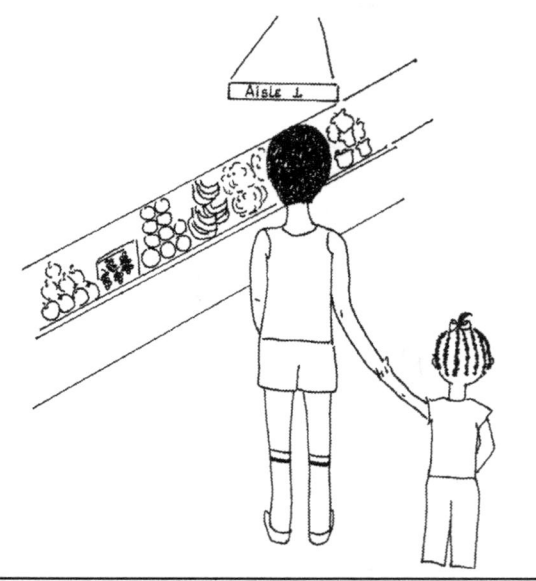

Mack said, "Do you see her from here?" The little girl shook her head.

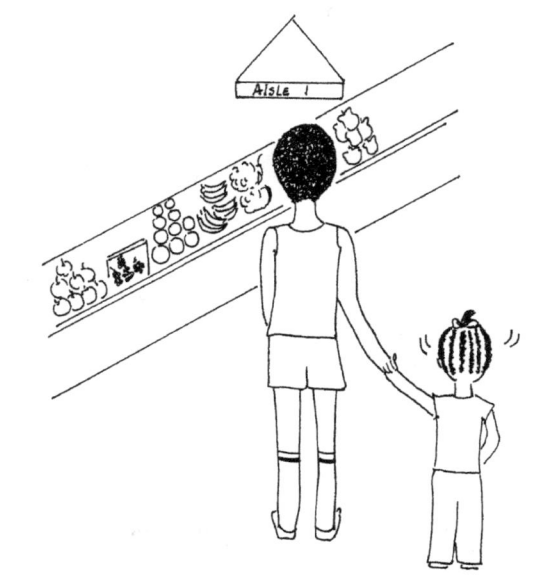

Then they walked to the second aisle. Mack said, "Now do you see her?" The little girl shook her head.

Mack Helps the Little Girl

Then they walked to the third aisle. Before Mack could even say anything, the little girl ran to her mother.

Her mother looked happy to see her, because she had been worried and looking for her daughter, too.

They were so happy to see each other that they forgot to say thank you to Mack. But he felt good just to see them happy and to know that he had helped the little girl.

Jimmy and Rolf-Ola Uglyzit

Once there was a boy whose name was Rolf-Ola Uglyzit.

When he went to school and told the people that his name was Rolf-Ola Uglyzit, all the children made fun of him and laughed at him and teased him.

And then they ran off and left him all alone.

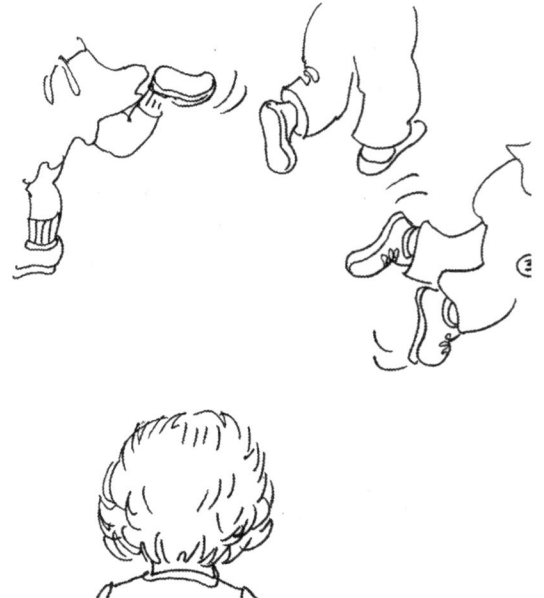

Jimmy and Rolf-Ola Uglyzit

He felt sad.

But then a boy named Jimmy came up to him and said, "Hi. My name is Jimmy. Do you want to play on the see-saw with me?"

And Rolf-Ola did, so they went and played on the see-saw.

Then Jimmy said, "Do you want to throw my football back and forth? Rolf-Ola said, "Yes, that would be nice!"

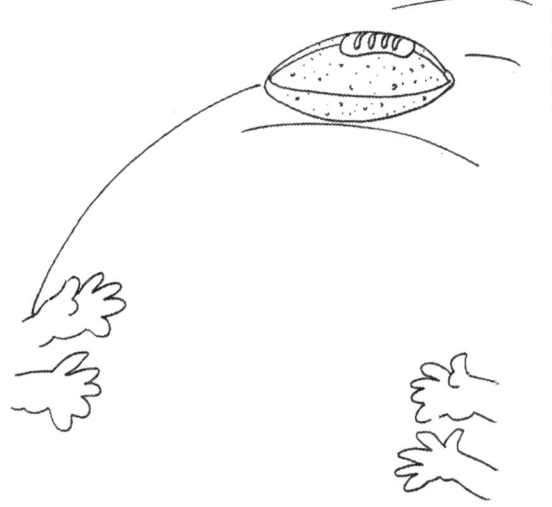

While they were throwing it, a kid came up and started teasing Rolf-Ola. Jimmy said, "Leave him alone, he's my friend."

The other kid was quiet for a while. Then he asked if he could throw the football too.

After they had finished playing, Jimmy felt really good, because he knew that he had made his new friend happy.

Frank Stops to Think

One time, there was a teenaged boy named Frank who was driving his car out in farm country.

There wasn't much traffic on the road. Frank got the urge to drive really fast just for the thrill of it.

But then he thought to himself, "Wait a minute. I should think about this before I do it. What could happen if I did go really fast?"

While he was thinking, a dog that he hadn't seen ran right out in front of his car.

Frank slammed on the brakes. There was a loud screech of tires as his car skidded across the road. Frank slowed down enough to miss hitting the dog, but just by an inch or two.

He thought to himself, "If I had been going any faster, I would have hit that dog. I'm glad I thought before I decided to go fast."

Frank was so glad not to have hit the dog that he stopped his car and just looked at him.

Frank Stops to Think

A boy came running out of the house nearby, having heard the screech of the tires. The boy looked really worried.

The dog ran to the boy. When the boy saw that the dog was OK, the boy looked very relieved.

Frank started his car and drove on. Frank thought, "I'll remember what happened today for a long time."

The Boy Goes to the Amazing People's Party

Once upon a time a boy got invited to a party that was to be given by some very amazing people in his neighborhood. He asked his mother if he could go.

His mother said, "Well, I see that the party lasts from three o'clock to six o'clock in the afternoon.

"Our family has to leave at five-thirty so we can catch a plane.

The Boy Goes to the Amazing People's Party

"If you go, you will have to leave before the party is over.

"You will get to go to the first two hours of the party, but then you will have to leave, no matter how good a time you are having. Do you think you can do that?

"Oh, yes," said the boy; and he felt good that he could go to the party with the amazing people even for part of the time.

The time came, and he went to the party. The amazing people first had some tame lions and tigers and elephants that the boy and his friends could take a ride on.

Illustrated Stories That Model Psychological Skills

And then they had a machine that would let everybody fly around in the air like Superman.

Then they let everybody play on a tightrope and a trapeze. There was a special net to catch you if you fell off.

The boy was having the best time he had ever had. Then the amazing people said, "Everything so far has just been very dull compared to what we're going to do next!"

The boy was very excited to hear that. Just at that moment, his mother came and said, "It's time to go."

The Boy Goes to the Amazing People's Party

He had the urge to whine and gripe and complain. But he remembered he had promised his mother that he would leave right away.

So, he told the amazing people, "Thank you so much for inviting me. I wish I could stay, but, as I told you earlier, I promised my mother."

The amazing people said good-bye. One of them told his mother, "Your son has quite a lot of self-control! Not many boys could leave like he did, without griping and complaining and whining.

"I think you have quite a son. I think we should invite him back again soon to do some more amazing and fun things."

Illustrated Stories That Model Psychological Skills

The Girl Waits for the Deer

A girl liked to walk around in the woods, to take hikes, and to camp out. One day when she was camping, she met an old man who was camping in the same area.

"Have you seen any deer or bears or foxes or possums?" he asked. "No," she said, "but I would like to."

"The animals get scared by noise or movement," he told her. "If you can be silent and still, you can see them."

Illustrated Stories That Model Psychological Skills

"You have to sit very still for a very long time. If you have picked the right spot, they will come around and you can see them."

He told her of a good spot to try. She thought, "I wonder if I can do it." At first it was hard for her to sit still very long.

She began to feel very cramped and restless. She had to get up to stretch. Then she reminded herself that it would take practice to do what she wanted to do.

She thought of how much she wanted to watch the animals. She thought, "I may have to put up with being uncomfortable if I want to watch them."

The Girl Waits for the Deer

She practiced for many days. Each day she was able to sit still a little bit longer. One day, finally, just as she was thinking of leaving her spot in the woods, she heard a soft sound nearby.

She didn't even turn her head to look. Only her eyes moved. She sat very still. In a minute, a mother deer with her baby deer came into sight.

She watched the deer and the fawn come to the stream and get a drink of water. After a good while they moved on, without ever seeing the girl.

At home, the girl was very happy. She told her parents and brothers and sisters what she had done and what she had seen.

She felt proud that she had been able to put up with sitting still so long. She knew that she could go back to that spot and see the deer again some other time.

Hal and the Contest at the Magic Kingdom

Once upon a time in a magic kingdom, the king decided to have a contest. A great prize was offered to the person who could pass a certain test.

Many people went to the castle and stood in line to take the test. A boy named Hal was one of them.

One by one, each person would go into a room. Each came out looking very hopeful.

But each one was told by the official tester, "You flunked. Sorry, bye-bye."

The boy ahead of Hal was named Ralph. Ralph went into the room. A man handed Ralph an envelope with the word "Directions" written on it. Also written on the envelope were the words, "Read this first, before doing or saying anything."

The man in the room said, "What's your name?"
The boy said, "My name is Ralph."

The man said, "Where is London?"
Ralph said, "It's in England, by the Thames River."
The man said, "How many things make a dozen?"
Ralph said, "Twelve."

Hal and the Contest at the Magic Kingdom

The man said, "Okay, go outside and find out how you did."
Ralph went outside and the other man said to him, "You flunked. So, bye-bye."

Hal then went into the room. As before, the man handed him an envelope bearing the words, "Directions. Read this first before doing or saying anything."
The man said to Hal, "What's your name?"

Hal was about to answer him, but then he said to himself, "Wait a minute. Let me think. The envelope says to read this before doing anything. He can wait a few seconds while I read it."

Hal opened the envelope and read what was written on the paper inside.

The paper said: "Directions: Here is how to pass the test. When anyone asks you a question that starts with 'What', do a little dance. When anyone asks you a question that begins with 'Where,' yawn and cough. When anyone asks you a question that starts with 'How,' do the silliest thing you can think of." 	Again the man asked Hal, "What is your name?" 
Hal said, "Here is your answer." Hal danced a little dance all around the floor. 	"That's a strange name," said the man. "Where is London?" At this, Hal gave a big yawn and a cough. 

Hal and the Contest at the Magic Kingdom

"Your time's up for that one," said the man. "How many things make a dozen?"

Hal remembered that he was supposed to do the silliest thing he could think of, so he acted like a pig who was turning into a monkey. He made faces and noises and hopped around in a very silly way.

"That is silly enough," said the man. "You have won. You were the first one who followed the directions."

So, Hal went before the King and there was a great ceremony. Everyone clapped for Hal!

It turned out that Hal's prize was ten free lessons from the king's daughter on how to use a computer. Hal had a great time.

Marilyn Becomes Friends With a Lonely Girl

Marilyn had lots of friends.

Marilyn sometimes liked to go by herself for a picnic in the park. She would sit and think about all the things that were good about her life and all the ways that she was lucky, and she would feel good.

A younger girl named Charlotte lived in the neighborhood. Charlotte was not at all pretty, and she also seemed to give people unfriendly looks. Marilyn knew that Charlotte didn't have friends and was left out of groups.

One day when Marilyn was going out for a walk, she saw Charlotte standing by herself, looking lonesome. Marilyn thought, "Charlotte doesn't seem happy. If I were unhappy and lonely, I would like it if someone would be friendly with me."

So, Marilyn said, "Hey Charlotte, I'm going for a walk. Do you want to come with me?"

Charlotte was so surprised that anyone would ask her to do something that she acted suspicious, rather than friendly. She said, "Well, I don't know…" She looked at Marilyn as if she were thinking, "You must be teasing me."

Marilyn did not let that bother her, and she kept on acting friendly. She said, "Do you ever go over to the park? It's nice on days like today."

Marilyn Becomes Friends with a Lonely Girl

Charlotte went along with Marilyn and when they got to the park, Marilyn gave Charlotte one of her sandwiches to eat. After a while, Charlotte didn't look suspicious anymore. She began to talk about herself and what went on in her life.

After that, Marilyn invited Charlotte to go for walks with her every now and then. Sometimes Charlotte told about sad things that had happened to her at home and at school. Once Marilyn put her arm around Charlotte's shoulder and comforted her while she cried.

At other times, Charlotte told Marilyn about the happy things that had happened.

Each time that Marilyn would take Charlotte with her, she felt good afterwards. She thought, "I'm glad I have the chance to make somebody feel better. And I enjoy her. I think she's learning how to be friendlier, so she'll find some other friends, too."

Illustrated Stories That Model Psychological Skills

Marilyn was out walking one day when she saw, from a long way off, a new girl who had just moved into the neighborhood. She thought to herself, "If I had just moved in, I'd want someone to come up to me and be friendly."

Marilyn walked toward the girl, but the girl turned around a corner.

Marilyn went in that direction, but before she got around the corner, she heard another girl's voice.

The other girl said, "Would you like for me to show you some of the good places to go in the neighborhood? We can take a walk together, if you'd like to?" The new girl said, "Sure. That would be nice."

Marilyn Becomes Friends with a Lonely Girl

Marilyn listened and peeked around the corner to see the two girls walking away. The girl who had been so friendly to the new girl was Charlotte!

After that, Marilyn saw Charlotte and this new girl together a lot. Sometimes she would join them on walks. Whenever she saw them, she felt proud that her friend was starting to get new friends of her own.

Illustrated Stories That Model Psychological Skills

The Amazing Person Helps Amos Not to Break Things

Amos had a bad habit of breaking things.

When he went to his friend's house, he picked up a vase and dropped it, and it smashed into a thousand pieces. He felt really bad.

When he was playing with an electronic game a friend had, he pushed a dial too hard and it broke off. The friend was so mad that he wouldn't let Amos play with any of his toys again.

The Amazing Person Helps Amos Not to Break Things

Amos felt so bad about these things that he went to see the amazing person who lived down the street. He could do all sorts of magic things.

The amazing person said, "I can help you with that problem. I'll put an imaginary man in your mind. He can tell you to watch out and keep you from breaking things."

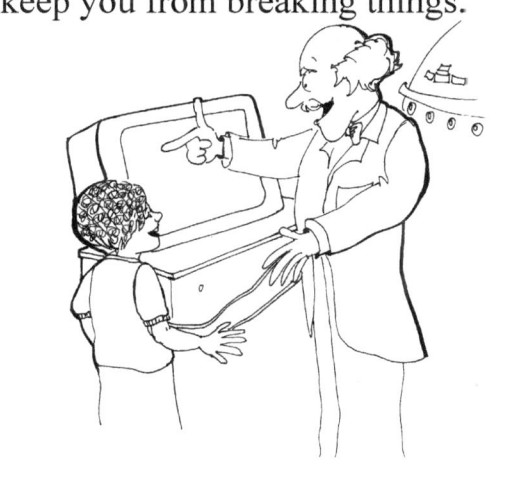

A few days later, Amos was looking at a briefcase that his father owned.

Amos couldn't get it open. He got the urge to use both his hands and feet and to pull on it as hard as he could.

But the imaginary man in Amos's head said, "Wait a minute, Amos. Think about what you are doing. You could break it if you do that."

So, Amos went to his father and said, "Could you show me how to open that briefcase that you said I could play with?"
And Amos's father said, "Sure."

His father showed him a button to push that made the case open very easily without forcing it.

The next day, a friend of Amos's showed him a model ship that he had put together. Amos held it in his hands.

The Amazing Person Helps Amos Not to Break Things

When Amos got through looking at it, he started to toss it down onto the floor. But the imaginary man in Amos's head said, "Hey, wait a minute. Think before you act!"

Then, Amos thought to himself, "Boy, I should put this down really gently, or it will break."

He put it down without breaking it. Then he said to the imaginary little man, "Thanks, little man. You're helping me out."
And he imagined that he heard, "You're welcome, Amos."

Illustrated Stories That Model Psychological Skills

Amos Stops to Think

Amos had gotten over a big problem with breaking things. He had solved his problem by learning to think before he acted.

One day, Amos's great-grandfather came to visit. The great-grandfather lived far away, and Amos had not seen him for a long time.

As the great-grandfather was reaching for a glass of water, he accidentally knocked the glass onto the floor, where it shattered into a hundred pieces.

Amos Stops to Think

The next day, Amos's great-grandfather was holding a plate of food. He accidentally dropped it. Even though it didn't break, the food spilled everywhere.

Amos had the urge to gripe at his great-grandfather and to say to him, "You're not thinking before you act! Stop and think before you reach for something!"

But Amos thought to himself, "Wait a minute. Do I want to say that? Let me think. I think my great-grandfather might have some other kind of problem. I will ask my mother some time later on."

So a little later on in the day, Amos went to his mother and asked, "Mother, what is wrong with great-grandfather that he drops things so much? Do you think it would help if I taught him to think before he acts?"

Amos's mother smiled at him and said, "I'm very glad you asked me about that before you said something to him. He has a disease that makes his fingers weak and can make his hands clumsy at times. That's why he drops things.

"You were right not to say anything right away. For all you knew, he could have been the sort of person who is easily embarrassed about this.

"But your great-grandfather doesn't mind talking about the disease he has. Ask him about it some time, and he'll tell you."

So Amos asked. His great-grandfather said, "Yes, it is bothersome, but I've learned to live with it pretty well." And then Amos and his great-grandfather had a nice talk.

Amos Stops to Think

Afterward, Amos said to himself, "I'm glad I thought before I spoke, and that I didn't gripe or get mad at him when he dropped things. My respectful talk let me get to know him better."

Illustrated Stories That Model Psychological Skills

Deborah Helps the Squirrel

Deborah was taking a walk. She saw a squirrel running across the street. A car was coming toward the squirrel.

The squirrel jumped for safety, but the car was coming too fast. The car hit the squirrel.

The people in the car didn't stop. Deborah ran to see what happened to the squirrel.

Deborah Helps the Squirrel

The squirrel was hurt but was not killed. Deborah thought that one of his back legs was broken.

Deborah was glad she had on very thick gloves, because she knew that hurt animals sometimes bite. Very slowly and gently she picked up the squirrel. The squirrel did not bite her.

Deborah took the squirrel back to her apartment. There she made a house for the squirrel out of a big wooden box. She made a bed for the squirrel out of some old rags. She called the squirrel Buddy.

Then Deborah made a splint for Buddy's hurt leg.

Illustrated Stories That Model Psychological Skills

Deborah fed nuts to Buddy.

Deborah gave Buddy water from an eye dropper.

Deborah spent a lot of time taking care of Buddy. After many days, Buddy got better, and was able to walk around again.

After more days, Buddy could hop and jump like any other squirrel.

Deborah Helps the Squirrel

Deborah thought, "He's gotten well. He won't be happy living in a house. I need to take him to the woods."

Deborah took Buddy to the middle of a big park. There were no cars and there were lots of trees with nuts on them.

Deborah let Buddy go. He very slowly climbed a tree. Deborah was sad to say good-bye to him.

Deborah went home alone. She knew she would miss her pet, but she felt good that she had done what was best for him.

After that, Deborah sometimes went back to the same place in the woods. One time, she saw Buddy again! He came down the tree and let her give him some nuts.

Deborah felt great that her squirrel was safe and happy in the woods.

Harry Helps His Dog

Harry Helps His Dog

Harry was at home by himself one Saturday.

All of a sudden he heard a big screech out in the street, and he looked out to see that a car had hit his dog! He ran outside, but the car had already driven away.

He felt very angry at the driver of the car, but he hardly had time to think about that, because he wanted to run to his dog and see what had happened.

His dog was named King. Luckily, King had not been run over but the car's bumper had scraped his hip and had given king a very, very bad cut. He was bleeding very fast.

Harry pressed right on the cut. He stopped the bleeding! Harry knew that with a cut this deep King would need to get to a veterinarian. But there was no one home to take him.

Harry said to himself, "Let's see. What could I do? I could try to walk and carry King to the Vet's, but that would be a long way and he'd probably lose a lot of blood along the way. I don't know if I could make it."

"I could call up friends who have a car and see if they can come and take us over to the vet's. Or, if no one can do that, I can take the money I've saved up and call a taxi cab and go to the vet's that way."

Harry Helps His Dog

"Or I could call up the vet's office and ask if they could come and pick us up."

Harry picked up his dog and went inside, still pressing down on the cut. King looked scared and hurt, but he seemed to understand that Harry would take care of him.

Harry went to the phone. He propped the receiver against his shoulder and dialed with one hand, while holding King's cut with the other hand.

First Harry called the vet's office, but the line was busy. Harry said, "At least I know there's someone there!" Harry couldn't reach any of his friends who had cars, so he called a taxi company.

When the taxi came, the driver was worried about getting blood on his cab, so Harry told him where to find some towels and newspapers to put on the seat.

The driver covered the seats, and Harry and King got in. The driver went straight to the vet's office.

Soon the vet had King's cut sewed up.

The vet said, "King will be OK. If you hadn't acted quickly and pushed down on the cut to stop the bleeding, King would have been a goner!"

Harry felt good about the choices he had made.

The Boy and the Complicated Present

Once upon a time a boy got a present from an uncle who lived far away. His uncle was very nice.

When the boy opened the package, all he saw was a bunch of pieces that needed to be fit together.

When he read the instructions that came with the present, he saw that he had been given something that could play chess with him, could help him make up songs, or could make lemonade or ice cream.

To get this amazing thing to work, he had to follow the instructions; there were 192 different steps in putting his present together.

He tried the first few steps and found that they were hard. He did something wrong and had to do it over. It took him a long time to finally get the first five steps of the instructions right. He had 187 more to go. He felt a little discouraged, but he kept on working.

He was invited to a party with all of his friends. He really had gotten tired of following all the instructions, but he wanted to show his friends his toy at the party. So he kept working.

Finally, he finished the last step. He had to do some of the steps over, but he finished just as the party was starting.

The Boy and the Complicated Present

He brought out his present and showed it to all of his friends. Everyone played chess on it and used it to make up songs. They thought it was a great toy.

And then the thing made lemonade and the best ice cream ever.

The boy felt good that he had the patience to put this amazing thing together.
He called his uncle to thank him. His uncle was proud that he had been able to put the thing together. His uncle said, "Maybe next year's present will be even harder!"

Illustrated Stories That Model Psychological Skills

The Boy and the Rattlesnake 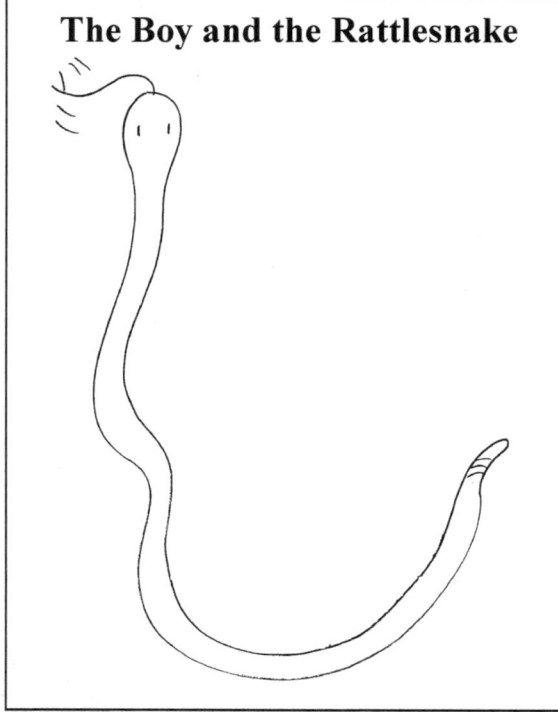	Once upon a time there was a boy who loved to go hiking and camping. 
One day while he was out in the woods, he lay down on the ground to take a rest. He dozed off to sleep. All of a sudden, he was awakened by a rattling sound. 	He opened his eyes to see a rattlesnake crawling across his legs! 

The Boy and the Rattlesnake

Most people would have screamed and jumped and run. This boy quickly decided that if he did that, he might scare the snake into biting him. So he lay perfectly still. The snake kept on crawling.

The snake slowly crawled across the boy, while the boy lay there and waited. It seemed to take a very long time for the snake to move away from the boy.

While the snake was moving, the boy watched the snake's tongue dart out of his mouth. He remembered that learning at school that the darting tongue did not mean that the snake was mad. The tongue helped the snake find his way.

As soon as the snake got so far away that he couldn't possibly swing back and bite the boy, the boy scrambled away to a safe distance.

Illustrated Stories That Model Psychological Skills

This sudden motion scared the snake; the snake coiled up into a position for biting. The boy thought, "I'll bet if I had jumped when he was closer to me, he would have bitten. I'm glad I was able to control myself and hold still."

The boy thought, "Should I try to kill this snake? Then he thought, "I'm grateful that he didn't bite me. I'll let him go in peace." The boy walked away and didn't see the snake again.

Jeff and the Broken Cup

As Jeff was walking though a department store carrying his jacket, he heard a crash.

He saw that his jacket had brushed against a bunch of cups that were hung up on a rack. He had knocked a cup off. It had broken into many pieces on the floor around him.

Jeff said to himself, "What do I do now? Let me think what my options are.

Illustrated Stories That Model Psychological Skills

"I could just walk along as if nothing happened.

"I could pick up the pieces of the cup.

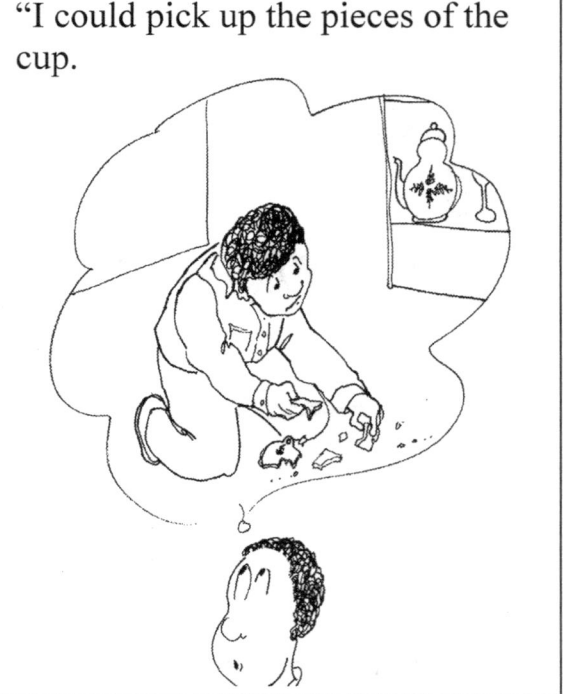

'Or I could go and tell the clerk that I broke a cup.

"Let's see. I wouldn't feel right about just walking away. If I pick up some of the pieces, that wouldn't really help anything. Someone will need to sweep up all the little pieces so no one walks on top of them.

Jeff and the Broken Cup

"It will be easier for people to see in the meantime if I leave the big pieces here too. If I tell the clerk, then he can get somebody to clean it up. He will probably ask me to pay for the cup, but I suppose that's only fair.

So Jeff told the clerk. The clerk said, "That's not the first cup that's been knocked off that rack. I think we should put the cups where they aren't so easy to knock over. Don't worry about it. They're cheap cups. You don't have to pay for it. I'll get somebody to clean it up."

Jeff was glad that the clerk was so nice. Jeff thought, "I made a good decision."

Illustrated Stories That Model Psychological Skills

Sheila Gets Separated From Her Mother

Sheila was with her mother in a shopping mall.

They were looking around in a department store.

All of a sudden, when Sheila looked around, her mother was not in sight.

Sheila Gets Separated From Her Mother

She looked around a little more and still didn't see her mother.

Sheila said to herself, "Now what options do I have? I could ask a person who works here to use a loudspeaker to tell my mother where to find me.

"Or I could go to the car and wait there.

"Or I could just walk around some more, without getting too far away from where I last saw her.

Illustrated Stories That Model Psychological Skills

"Or I could just stay right here and wait for her to find me."

Then Sheila said to herself, "If I go to the car, she'll probably spend a lot of time looking before she gets there, and she'll probably be worried or irritated.

"If I have it announced over the loud speaker, she will probably hear it and find me.

"If I look around this area for a while longer, she'll come back or I'll find her. I think I'll do that for a while longer. If that doesn't work, I'll ask the people at the store for help."

Sheila Gets Separated From Her Mother

After Sheila had looked around for just a little bit longer, she found her mother not far away.

Gina and the Gymnastics Meet

Gina had a long homework assignment to do.

Just as she was starting to do it, a friend of hers called and said, "Hey, do you want to see a gymnastics meet tonight? My family is going, and you can come with us."

Gina really wanted to go. She liked doing cartwheels and somersaults and trying to walk on her hands and doing tricks on a tree limb.

Gina and the Gymnastics Meet

She wanted to see the people who could do all these things very well. She had seen gymnastics on TV, and she wanted to see it in person.

But then she thought about her homework assignment. She told her friend, "Can you hold on just a second? I need to think about this."

Then Gina said to herself, "What are my options? I could stay home and do my homework and try to see the gymnastics meet some other time. If I did that, I wouldn't get to have the fun with my friends and it might be a while before I get a chance to go again.

"Or, I could go to the meet and then stay up late doing my homework. Or I could go, and then get up really early to do my homework tomorrow morning.

Illustrated Stories That Model Psychological Skills

"Or I could go to the meet and not do my homework. If I did that, I would feel bad tomorrow when I hadn't done my work.

"If I try to go to the meet and do my homework, I might be very sleepy tomorrow, but I can go to bed early tomorrow night.

"I think what I want to do is to go and to do my homework after I get home. I can also work some before the meet starts if I work really fast." So, Gina told her friend, "Yes, I'd like to go with you."

So, Gina did as she decided. When she got home, she was sleepy, but she stayed awake and finished her homework. It was hard to get up the next morning.

Gina and the Gymnastics Meet

That night, Gina did her homework right away and went to bed early. The next morning, she felt relaxed and refreshed. She felt good about her decisions.

Alex Helps The Animals

Alex had a job cutting the grass for Mr. LeCron. Mr. LeCron lived in a big house with a big yard with lots of trees. The window shades of his house were always closed. No one had ever been inside the house. No one knew much about Mr. LeCron.

Mr. LeCron would sometimes give Alex errands to do. Mr. LeCron also left money lying around, but Alex never took any of it.

When a neighborhood dog came around, Alex would always take a minute to pet the dog. He loved animals.

Alex Helps the Animals

Alex noticed that Mr. LeCron seemed to be watching him very closely when he petted the dog. Alex liked Mr. LeCron. Mr. LeCron always kept his word on everything he said to Alex.

One day, Mr. LeCron said, "Alex, you always come on time; you always follow my directions; and you seem like a kind, loving person to animals. And I also trust your parents.

"Do you think I can trust you to do something very important for me? I'll pay you well, but you must keep a secret from everyone except your parents."

Alex decided to hear more about this secret job. Mr. LeCron said to him, "I'll take you into my house, but even if you decide not to take the job, you must never tell anyone what you see in here."

Illustrated Stories That Model Psychological Skills

Alex promised. Mr. LeCron took him into the house. Alex was amazed by what he saw. Mr. LeCron lived in only a very few rooms. The rest of the house was a huge open room.

There were plants all over everywhere -- grass growing on the ground, tall trees, bushes; it was just like a jungle garden, except that there were lights on the ceiling up above instead of a sun.

Then Alex saw the animals. There was a family of chimpanzees and some deer. Alex could not believe how cute and lovable they were. The monkeys came to Mr. LeCron and hugged him, and the deer nuzzled against him.

Mr. LeCron said, "These are the animals that live here with me. Your job would be to take care of them when I am out of town. Do you think you can do it?"

Alex Helps the Animals

Alex took the job. Mr. LeCron would leave town very suddenly without ever saying where he was going. Alex would then go every day to feed and take care of the animals.

Alex was patient and gentle. Gradually the animals began to trust him. The chimpanzees would run up to him and jump into his arms and he would hug them. Alex spent a lot of time with a baby chimpanzee.

The deer got so used to Alex that they would eat out of Alex's hand and let him rub their fuzzy noses.

Alex always made sure that the animals had enough to eat. He loved to watch them eat. Sometimes it seemed to him that they even smiled at him as he fed them.

Even when Mr. LeCron was in town, Alex would go and see the animals often and help with the work. He loved to pet them and he loved to feed them. Alex kept the secret. Mr. LeCron could not even tell him why the secret had to be kept.

Alex wondered about Mr. LeCron. He wondered if Mr. LeCron had to keep the secret because he was doing something wrong. But Alex never found out anything.

Years passed. Alex grew up and moved away. One day, on a trip to another city, he took a walk through a beautiful park. There he noticed a man and a woman and two children having a good time together. The man looked familiar; as Alex went closer, he recognized Mr. LeCron.

Alex went up and spoke to him. Mr. LeCron was very glad to see Alex. He said, "This is my wife and these are our children."

Alex Helps the Animals

Alex and Mr. LeCron spent a long time talking. Mr. LeCron said, "Alex, I can tell you now why the animals were such a secret. At the time you worked for me, I was doing detective work against organized crime groups, like the Mafia.

"If I had had a wife and children at that time, they would have been in danger, so I didn't have a family then. I stayed pretty much to myself. I even kept the place where I lived a secret.

"But, I was always the type of person who needed to have someone to take care of and to love and to protect," Mr. LeCron continued. "It would have been impossible to have a family and keep my family a secret, but I could have animals and keep them a secret. They were like children to me, all during the time I was in that dangerous job.

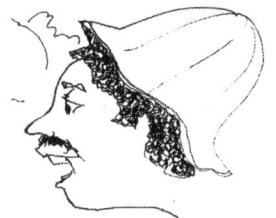

"I didn't like going out of town and leaving them. I worried about them until I learned to trust you. You took good care of them, as well as I did, and you always kept the secret."

Alex said, "I loved those animals, too." Then Mr. LeCron told Alex about some of the things that had happened while he was a detective.

Alex felt good to hear the reason for the secret after all the years. Mr. LeCron looked happy, sitting with his arm around his wife, watching his children play. Alex felt happy, too.

The Girl Handles It When Her Friend Leaves

The Girl Handles It When Her Friend Leaves

A girl invited a friend to visit her house for the afternoon.

They had a good time making mud pies.

They washed the dog.

Illustrated Stories That Model Psychological Skills

They thought up new inventions. They were just about to make a great discovery.

Suddenly the friend looked at her watch and said, "I must go home."

The girl wanted her friend to stay longer. She had the urge to gripe and complain at her friend. She felt mad at her friend for having to leave so soon. But she thought, "If I get upset, my friend will be less likely to come over the next time."

So, she just said, "Thanks for coming! I wish you didn't have to leave so soon." The friend said, "I wish that too, but my parents want me home early this evening."

The Girl Handles It When Her Friend Leaves

When the friend left, the girl had a good time playing by herself. She thought, "I'm glad I was able to let my friend leave without getting upset!"

Jean Handles it When Patty Moves Away

Jean moved into a new town. She didn't know anyone.

While walking around in the neighborhood, she met Patty.

Jean and Patty became best friends. They would get together almost every afternoon.

Jean Handles It When Patty Moves Away

They spent the night with each other.

They talked to each other on the phone and told each other all about what they had been thinking and feeling.

If ever Jean needed to borrow something, she would go to Patty. When Patty couldn't understand how to do a math problem, she would ask Jean. When Patty had a problem with another person, she would talk to Jean about it.

Then one day, Patty had something sad to tell Jean. "My father's job is moving. I'll have to move to another state."

Jean was very sad. She cried some and told Patty how much she would miss her. She had the urge to mope around for a long time, but she said to herself, "Well, this is a chance to practice putting up with something that I don't want."

After Patty moved away, Jean was almost afraid to make more friends for fear that they would leave too. She reminded herself, "I can take that too, if it happens." So she made some new friends and gradually started having more fun with them.

Jean didn't forget Patty. She and Patty wrote to each other often. They also got to talk on the phone long distance.

One day, Patty's family came back to visit. Jean and Patty were able to see each other again. They hugged each other and spent a long time talking and laughing.

Jean Handles It When Patty Moves Away

When it came time for Patty to leave again, Jean said, "We can feel bad that it's time to go, or we can feel good that we are still able to see each other and keep in touch." They decided to feel good. They kept on being friends for many years.

Illustrated Stories That Model Psychological Skills

Frank and Zane Go Running

Frank and Zane were good friends.

They took a cross-country run together. They went to the woods and ran across the trails for a long time.

Frank and Zane were both in good shape, but Frank was in especially good shape.

Frank and Zane Go Running

Zane said, "Frank, it seems that you never even get tired or even have to breathe very hard. I don't know how you do it."

Frank said, "Thank you." He remembered all the times that he had kept on running even though he was very tired. He felt good that he had been able to put up with feeling tired and out of breath without quitting.

Frank and Zane took a shower and changed clothes. They realized they were very hungry. They went to a restaurant together and ordered some food.

Before the food came, Zane remembered that he needed to call his mother on the phone. He left to make his call. Just after he left, the waitress brought their food to the table.

Illustrated Stories That Model Psychological Skills

Frank felt like starting to eat, but in his family, there was a custom that no one started eating until everyone could start together. Frank was very, very hungry and the food smelled great. But Frank said to himself, "I will put up with waiting, so that Zane and I can eat together."

Zane was on the phone a long time. When he finally came back to the table, he noticed that Frank had not touched his food. Zane said, "Frank, have you been waiting for me so that we could eat together? I'm amazed that you have so much self-control! How could you sit here and not eat when the food smells so good and you're so hungry?"

"It's not so hard," Frank said. "I enjoy it more when people can eat together."
Zane said, "I've never seen anybody with such self-discipline! Now I know why you're such a good runner."

Freddy and the Explosive

Freddy and the Explosive

Freddy was out for a walk with his father.

They were walking out in the country. They came to an open field with huge rocks. There were workmen nearby and some signs that Freddy couldn't read.

Freddy saw something on the ground that looked interesting. He ran over to pick it up. But his father said, "Stop!"

Illustrated Stories That Model Psychological Skills

Freddy's father said, "Freddy, don't go near that. Come here right away!"

Freddy still wanted to see the thing on the ground, but he reminded himself that there were lots of things he wanted to do that he would have to put up with not doing.

He returned to where his father was standing and did as he was told. He said to himself, "There are plenty of other things I can do to have fun, even though I'd like to pick up the mysterious thing on the ground."

He soon found out what the mysterious thing was. A rock fell on the thing and there was an explosion. The thing on the ground blew up and rocks went flying all over everywhere.

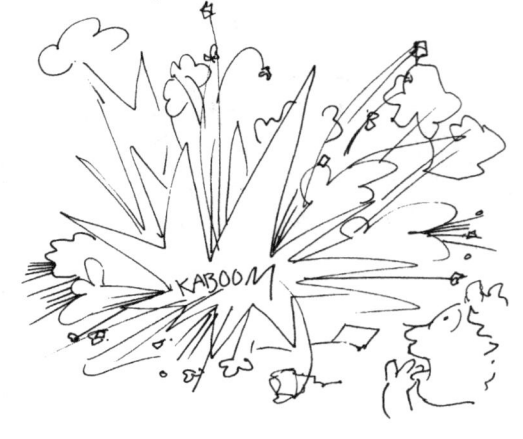

Freddy and the Explosive

Freddy's father said, "That is why I didn't want you to go over and play in that area, Freddy. They use explosives around here, and that thing you were looking at is called a blasting cap."

Freddy felt glad that his father knew what was dangerous. Freddy felt very glad that he had obeyed his father and had put up with not doing what he had felt like doing.

James Lets the Little Boy Play with the Basketball

James spent a lot of time playing basketball with other boys his age on the neighborhood playground.

A little boy James knew was there with his mother, watching them play. James said to him, "Hey, fellow, how're you doing?" The little boy smiled and looked pleased to be noticed.

After the game was over, the little boy was still watching them. James thought he looked interested in the basketball, so he offered the ball to the little boy and said, "Do you want to try it?"

James Lets the Little Boy Play with the Basketball

The little boy took the basketball and tried to throw it toward the basket, but he could barely get it more than a foot into the air.

James said, "Hmm, that's a little hard for someone your size. Here, let's see if you can do this instead." James took an old can that someone had left lying around and set it on top of a little wall.

James said, "Let's see if you can throw the ball and knock the can off the wall -- like this." And James threw the ball to knock the can off.

Then the little boy took the basketball and threw it at the can. The second time he tried, he knocked the can off. And James clapped for him and said, "Hooray! You did it!"

Illustrated Stories That Model Psychological Skills

The boy smiled and looked pleased and clapped his own hands. James said to himself, "I get a kick out of seeing him have a good time." They played together at this game some more.

The little boy's mother had been watching. She said to James, "He loves it when you older boys pay some attention to him." James felt good that he had helped the boy have a good time.

George and the One-Way Street

One time a boy named George was about to walk over to a friend's house across the street.

The street they lived on was a one-way street, so cars came from only one direction. George looked in that direction and saw that no cars were coming, so he started to run across the street.

But then he said to himself, "Wait a minute. Let me stop and think. I'd better stay in the habit of looking both ways."

So, he looked the other way. There was a car coming in the wrong direction down the one-way street!

As the car passed, George waved his hands and yelled, "Hey, stop!"

The fellow driving the car was named Harry. When Harry saw George waving his hands and yelling, his first urge was to yell back, "Oh, bug off!"

But then he thought to himself, "Wait a minute, let me think about this. Maybe he's trying to help me or maybe he needs help. I'll stop and see what he wants."

George and the One-Way Street

Harry stopped. He was very surprised when George told him he was going the wrong way on a one-way street. "Thanks for telling me," Harry said. "I didn't see the sign."

Harry turned around. He was glad he had thought before he acted. He wondered what would happened if he had just hollered at George and driven on.

Judy Makes a Plan About Her Dog

Judy came home one afternoon very tired. She had just started running on the cross-country team and had been running all afternoon.

She also had been up late the night before, studying for a test. And she also felt grumpy, because someone had said some things to her that weren't nice.

When she got home, her dog Arnold was inside, jumping around, wagging his tail and wanting Judy to take him outside. Judy looked at him and at first she thought, "Oh no! Here's something else I have to do."

Judy Makes a Plan About Her Dog

But she then thought to herself, "Well, he is my dog and I want to take care of him." She looked at his face and she could see how much he wanted her to take him outside.

Arnold had been cooped up in the house all day long. Judy said to herself, "He wants to go out and run even more than I want to go and lie down."

So, Judy took Arnold out. As soon as he stepped outside the door, he looked as happy as he could be, just as Judy had known he would be.

She watched him running around sniffing everything. She was glad she had taken him out. She loved to see him having fun.

Judy thought to herself, "He needs to run more. How can I let him do that?" Then Judy got an idea.

The next day, she told the running coach all her reasons for wanting to run home quickly before cross-country practice to get Arnold and take him running with her.

The coach thought about Judy's idea and decided that the girls on her team might feel safer if a dog ran with them. So she said to Judy, "Yes, we can give it a try."

From that day on, Arnold ran cross-country with Judy's team every afternoon. He got lots of attention from the other girls on the team before and after they ran. Judy could tell that he just loved the whole thing and that made Judy feel great.

Peter and His Grandmother

Peter and His Grandmother

Peter's grandmother lived with him and his family. Ever since Peter was a baby, his grandmother had done nice things for him.

She had taken him outside in his stroller. When he had learned to walk, she had taken him to the park. She had watched him while he walked around.

When he had looked at the squirrels, bushes, water fountains, and people, she had followed him around to make sure he was safe.

At night, his grandmother had read him stories and had sung songs to him.

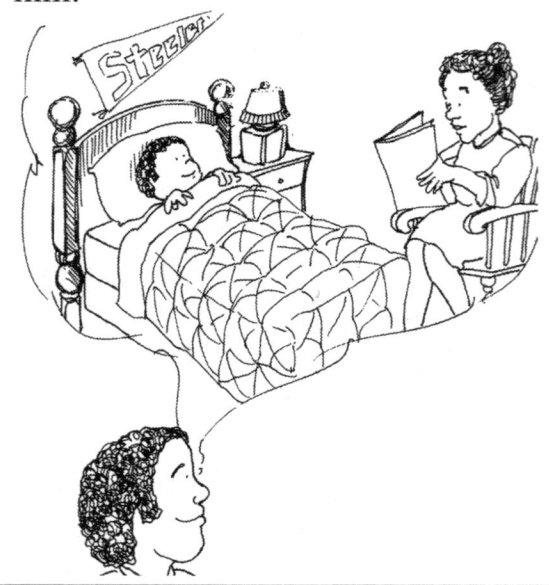

Before he learned to tie his shoes, he had gone to her; she would tie them for him. She was the one who finally taught him to tie his shoes for himself.

As the years went by, Peter's grandmother got a disease that no doctor could cure. She gradually got worse and worse at remembering things. Because of this disease, she sometimes said or did strange things.

One night, she was trying to wash dishes. She picked up a box of oatmeal and started to pour it into the sink. Peter noticed this and said, "Wait a minute, grandmother."

Peter and His Grandmother

He very gently took the oatmeal box from her hand and put the box of soap in its place.

He stood beside her and let her wash the dishes, because he knew it made her feel good to be doing something useful. When she needed any help, he gave it. Peter's grandmother saw this and smiled at Peter.

Another time, Peter's grandmother was looking around in the hall closet, saying something to herself about orange juice. Peter said to her, "Do you want some orange juice?"

She said, "Yes," and he led her to the refrigerator and opened it for her. He watched to make sure that she found the orange juice, and gave her a cup for her to pour herself some.

Another time, she was talking about someone who had been dead for a long time. She seemed worried that this person wouldn't have enough money to take care of himself.

No matter what anybody said, she worried. Peter said to himself, "I'll bet I can get the worrying out of her mind by singing some songs for her." So he did, and it worked.

One time, Peter's mother said, "Peter, you do such a good job of being patient and loving with your Grandmother. Do you remember how she was before she got sick?"

Peter said, "Yes, I remember. She was patient with me and would follow me around to make sure I didn't get into trouble. She would sing to me and help me. Now that she needs the same thing, I feel good that I can help her."

Peter and His Grandmother

Later on, Peter's mother told Peter's father what Peter had said. His father smiled and said, "Our son is a pretty amazing boy."

The Boy and His Bow and Arrows

A boy was interested in archery. He wanted to save his money to buy a bow and arrows.

His father said to him, "Son, you can buy them, but you have to remember that a bow and arrow can be dangerous. You should never, ever point the arrow in the direction of anyone else, even if you are just joking.

"If you do point the arrow toward someone, you will have to give up the bow and arrows for one whole year, even after you bought them yourself."

The Boy and His Bow and Arrows

The boy thought that this was fair. He spent a long time working and saving his money, and finally he had enough to buy the bow and arrows.

When he bought them, he said to himself, "There were lots of other things that I could have bought with my money, but I saved it. I went without a lot of snacks and games and other things so I could buy this bow and arrows.

"But now, I am glad I put up with going without those other things. Having my bow and arrows is worth it."

He made himself a target out of some bales of hay and a cloth cover, and he had a good time shooting.

Sometimes he would invite his friends over. His father would watch them shoot and would shoot with them.

One day, the boy forgot his promise to his father. He and his friend were playing. The boy laughed and pointed the arrow at his friend. He drew the string back a little bit.

The friend laughed too, because he knew the boy wouldn't really shoot him.

However, the boy's father said, "Son, you have done what I told you not to do; you have pointed an arrow at someone. I will have to take the bow and arrows away from you. Don't ask me to give them back to you."

The Boy and His Bow and Arrows

The boy knew his father was right. The boy felt very ashamed of himself, because he knew that he could have accidentally let go and hurt his friend.

The boy was very disappointed. He enjoyed the archery very much, but he decided that he could put up with not being able to shoot.

He got interested in other things and had a good time doing them. Still, he wished that he could shoot again. He got the urge to ask his father if he could shoot, but he remembered that his father had told him not to ask. So he did not.

Months passed. One day his father said to him. "Please come with me, son." They went to a closet, and his father took out the bow and arrows.

His father said, "I think you will not point it at anyone again. Do you think so too?" The boy answered, "I know I won't point it at anyone again."

Happily, he took the bow and arrows from his father. Then he noticed the calendar on the wall nearby. The date looked familiar. He remembered that it was one year ago, to the day, when he had pointed the arrow at his friend.

The boy was thankful that his father cared enough about him to teach him to use the bow and arrows safely.

The Boy and the Football

The Boy and the Football

A boy had a friend over to visit at his house. The boy had a new football and really wanted to try it out. He said to his friend, "Come on! Let's throw the football some!"

His friend was not at all interested in throwing the football and said, "I really don't like to throw a football. I was really hoping to play on the tire swing over there. Can you do it with me?"

The boy tried to persuade his friend to play football, but the friend hated football. The boy started to get upset and irritated, but then he reminded himself that sometimes he needed to put up with doing thing that were not his first choice.

He played on the rope swing with his friend, and pretty soon he was having a great time.

The next day, he called up another friend and asked if he wanted to throw the football, and that friend did. He had a good time that day. He was glad that he had also been able to enjoy his other friend the day before.

Ted Waits for his Friends to Finish Playing

Ted was at the park.

Ted saw a couple of older friends, named Bill and Doug. They were playing chess. Ted wanted them to race with him.

Ted ran up to them and said, "Hi Bill and Doug!"
They looked up briefly and said, "Hi." But they were concentrating on their game. They didn't want to pay attention to him.

At first, Ted felt mad at them for not paying attention to him. He got the idea of grabbing a few of their chess pieces and running away. That would make them race after him.

But then Ted imagined what would happen after that. Bill and Doug would be mad at him for spoiling their game. They would not want him around. And the next time they saw him, they still might not want to play with him.

So, Ted said to himself, "Maybe I'll just watch them for a while." So he stood and studied the game. He didn't know how to play chess, but he tried to figure it out.

Ted watched for a very long time. He figured out that the men moved differently. Some moved straight ahead, and others moved diagonally.

Ted Waits for his Friends to Finish Playing

Finally the game ended and Bill said to Doug, "That was a good game, Doug. Thanks for playing. I have to go now." And Bill left.

Doug said to Ted, "Do you want to play?"
Ted said, "I don't know how. I was just trying to figure it out."

Doug said, "I'll show you a little bit about how to do it. It's a hard game." So, Ted paid very close attention. He tried to remember as much as he could.

After a while, Doug looked at his watch. He said, "I have to go, too, Ted."

Illustrated Stories That Model Psychological Skills

Ted said, "Thanks for showing me how to play, Doug." Ted was glad that he had waited. He had learned a lot and he knew that in a while he might be able to play chess himself.

The Boy Who Could Put Up With His Parents' Paying Attention to Something Else

The Boy Who Could Put Up With His Parents' Paying Attention to Something Else

One time there was a boy who looked very ordinary. If you looked at him, you would not know that he had an amazing ability.

One day some travelers came through town. They heard that the boy was an expert at putting up with his parents' paying attention to someone else. They decided to go and see for themselves.

The travelers went to the boy's house. They said to his parents, "Please, we have come to see the boy who can put up with his parents' paying attention to something else. May we visit you for a while?"

Illustrated Stories That Model Psychological Skills

The boy's mother and father invited the travelers to come in. They sat down and talked with the travelers.

The boy came up to them. He had wanted his parents to play a game with him. His parents introduced him to the travelers. He said to himself, "Well, they seem to want to talk to the guests. So, I'll wait until later." And while he was waiting, he picked up a magazine and looked at the pictures in it.

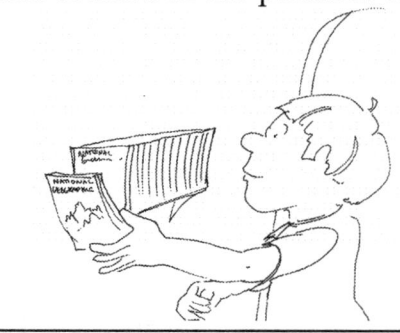

His parents went on talking to the travelers for a while. The boy decided that if he didn't get to play the game with his parents, he would draw a picture.

Then one of the travelers said to the other, "Hey, he's doing it right now!" He's putting up with his parents' paying attention to something else, namely us! Amazing!"

The Boy Who Could Put Up With His Parents' Paying Attention to Something Else

At that moment, the phone rang. The boy's father went to answer it. Then the OTHER phone rang. This family had two separate phone lines. The mother went to answer it. One of the travelers said, "Surely he won't be able to handle this."

The other traveler said, "No, surely he'll bug them at least once, if they're on the phone very long."

The boy saw that both his parents were on the phone. So he said to himself, "I can handle this with no problem." And he went on drawing.

After a while he thought to himself, "I'll go over and see if the guests want company." So he went and stood near them.

Illustrated Stories That Model Psychological Skills

But they were speaking among themselves as though they were very interested in something. So, he said to himself, "They don't look like they want to be interrupted just now."

So he decided to make up a story about his toy people.

The toy people did some very interesting things.

The boy's parents spoke on the phone for a very long time. When they got off the phone, the travelers were truly amazed. They said, "He did it! I don't believe what I just saw!" One of them was so amazed that he jumped up and did a back flip.

The Boy Who Could Put Up With His Parents' Paying Attention to Something Else

The travelers asked the boy, "How did you do it? How did you do such a good job of putting up with your parents' paying attention to something else?"

The boy said, "It wasn't very hard. I just reminded myself that I could handle it, and then did something fun by myself."

The travelers said, "We just have to give you a big round of applause for that performance. That was wonderful.

"We've never seen anybody do such a good job of putting up with his parents' paying attention to something else! Bravo!" The boy took a bow.

Illustrated Stories That Model Psychological Skills

After the travelers had gone, the boy got to play catch with his father. He was glad that he had been able to wait.

The Boy Learns About Champions' Mistakes

The Boy Learns About Champions' Mistakes

A boy was trying to learn to do lots of things. He was trying to learn to read, to play soccer, to play the piano and to ice skate.

He had a problem. He thought his problem was that he made mistakes. Very often when he was reading, he would miss a word or not know what a word was.

When he did this, he would feel bad and want to quit trying to read. He would say, "I want to do something else."

Or when he was practicing soccer, very often when he would kick the ball, the ball wouldn't go where he wanted it to go. He would think, "I'll quit doing this and take a walk instead."

Or when he was playing the piano, often he would play the wrong notes. He would think, "That sounded terrible. I'll watch TV instead."

One day the boy was walking in his neighborhood and he saw his friend, the Amazing Person.

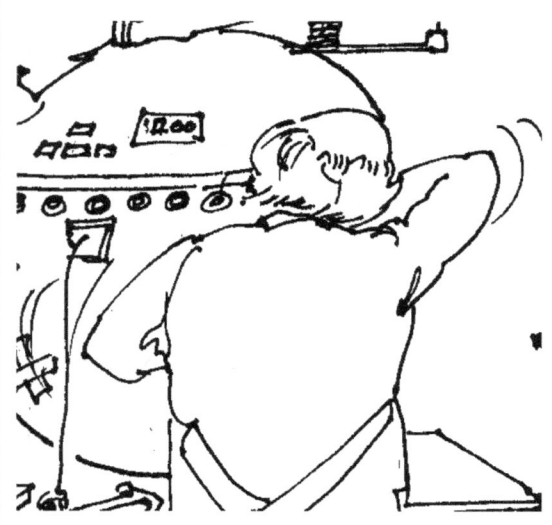

The Amazing Person was just finishing an invention made out of recycled televisions, computers and telescopes. The boy said, "Hi, Amazing Person. What are you finishing now?"

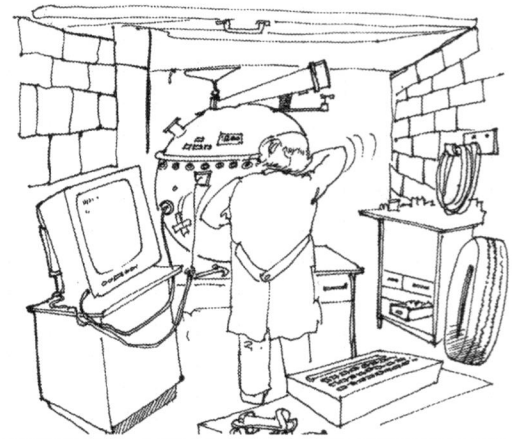

The Boy Learns About Champions' Mistakes

The Amazing Person said, "It's a great device. It allows you to capture light rays that went hurling off into space a long time ago and see things that happened back then.

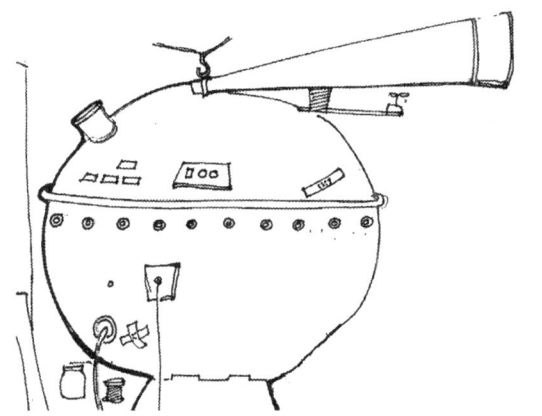

"It lets you see the past in the present! There are probably all sorts of problems that this machine will solve. Just name a problem, and we'll see if it can solve it!"

The boy said, "I don't think it can solve my problems with learning to read, play soccer, play the piano, and ice skate."

But the Amazing Person said, "Let's try! Tell me about them." So the boy said, "I have a problem; it's that I make mistakes." And he told the Amazing Person about the mistakes he made.

When he heard about this, the Amazing Person was very excited. He said, "Hey! I think we can solve this problem! The problem you have isn't that you make mistakes.

"It's that you let your mistakes discourage you from trying again and again! But why should you believe that just from my telling you? Let's see if I can convince you with my new machine! Would you like to try it out?"

The boy said, "Yes."
The Amazing person said, "OK, let's see. What we need to do is to capture the light rays of a soccer champion. We'll look at him just when he was starting out and see if he made mistakes or not."

All of a sudden, there came onto the screen a movie of a famous diving champion, practicing diving! The Amazing Person said, "Well, we almost got it. But let's see what this is."

The Boy Learns About Champions' Mistakes

As they watched, they saw the diving champion go off the board. He flopped, right onto his belly! The boy said, "Ouch! I bet that hurt! I bet he'll call it quits for the day."

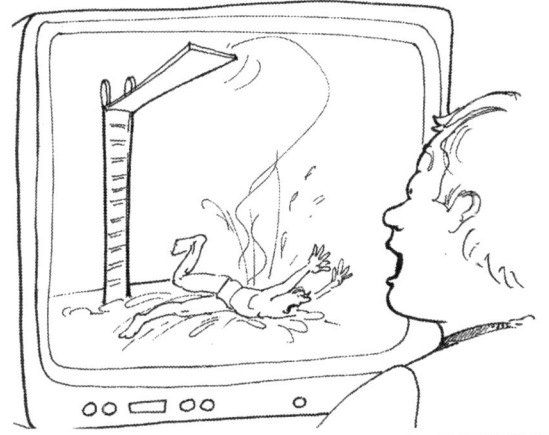

But the diving champion got out of the water and talked to his coach. All his coach said was, "Do you know what to do differently next time?"

The champion nodded and said, "Yes, I need to stay tucked in a ball longer." The coach said, "Rehearse it in your mind a few times before you try again."

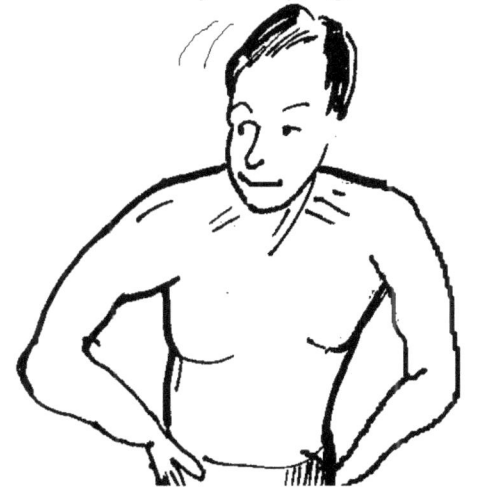

The champion stood on the board and concentrated for a while. He was picturing in his mind what he would do.

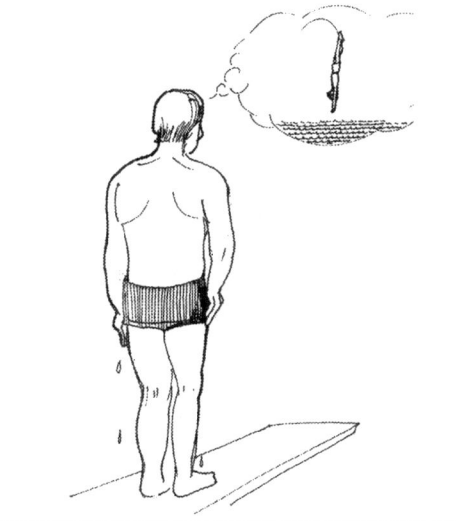

The next time, the diving champion went a little too far in the other direction. This time he almost flopped over onto his back. The boy said, "This just isn't his day. Maybe he should try it another day."

But the champion got up and practiced in his mind again, and he tried the dive again. And he kept on and on and on.

After he had done it twenty-five times, the Amazing Person said, "Let's put this on fast-forward." The boy and the Amazing Person counted over a hundred times that the champion practiced the dive.

The champion kept making mistakes, but they got less and less frequent. When the champion did a really good dive, he got out of the water with a big smile on his face. The Amazing Person said, "He feels really good now, doesn't he?"

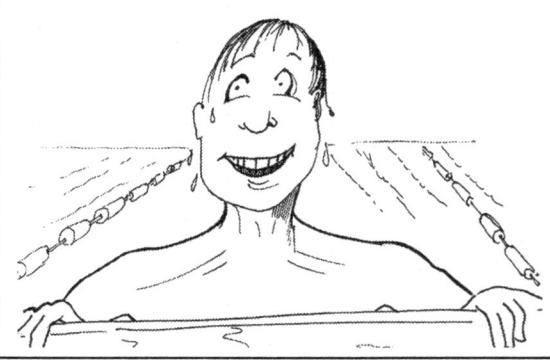

The Boy Learns About Champions' Mistakes

Then they turned the machine to ultra-fast-forward, until they got to the time of the champion's first diving competition. "He's practiced so much, surely he won't make any mistakes here," said the boy.

But the very first dive that the champion did, he walked out to the end of the board just to test the springiness of the board. He jumped up and down a couple of times and lost his balance.

The champion fell into the pool without even diving! All the people watching the diving meet laughed! The boy said, "After all that practice! Surely he's so embarrassed that he will just go home and try it another day!"

But the champion got out and walked to the diving board again, concentrating very hard. Then he did his dive and did a very good job of it. The boy said, "Wow! What a pretty move! He looks happy now."

Illustrated Stories That Model Psychological Skills

After they had finished watching, the boy said to the Amazing Person, "I think I catch on!" He made tons of mistakes! In fact, he probably made more diving mistakes in one afternoon than most people make in their whole lives!"

"But each time he made one, he would try to rehearse in his mind how to do it better the next time, and would try it again."

The amazing person said, "Yes! In fact, champions probably make more mistakes than other people, because they practice so much more. But when our diving champion finally got his dive right, he felt really good!

"But let's see if that's also true for other champions and not just this one. Let's see if we can find that soccer champion we were looking for."

The Boy Learns About Champions' Mistakes

When the next person came onto the screen, the Amazing Person said, "I was trying to get a soccer player, but instead I got a champion scholar! This college guy is a winner of a prize in mathematics!"

"He did better on the math test than anyone else in the whole state! He made up lots of math ideas that were useful to lots of people, too, and he published it in an article!"

Then they looked at pictures of the champion scholar when he was learning to count and when he was learning to add and learning to solve problems. The boy said, "Wow! It's just the same as the diver!"

"But when he gets the wrong answer, that just seems to make him more curious to find the right answer. He keeps searching for it. And when he finds it, he gets really happy!"

Then they looked at pictures of a champion horseback rider falling off the horse many, many times before learning how to keep from falling. The champion kept rehearsing what she was going to do differently the next time, getting back onto the horse, and trying again.

When she finally stayed on well, she had a big smile on her face.

And they saw a pair of champion figure skaters practicing. They knocked each other over a few times and both landed on the ice. But then they talked about how to do it better the next time, and they tried again.

When they finally did it well, they were so happy that they hugged each other.

The Boy Learns About Champions' Mistakes

The boy said, "Thanks, Amazing Person. I think I learned something important from this. I think I'm going to go home and practice some of the things I've been learning. What are you going to do?"

And the Amazing Person said, "I'm really curious about why my machine won't give me just the right sort of champion when I ask it to. I've got an idea about how to fix it."

As the boy left, he saw the Amazing person tinkering with his new invention, trying again and again to get it right.

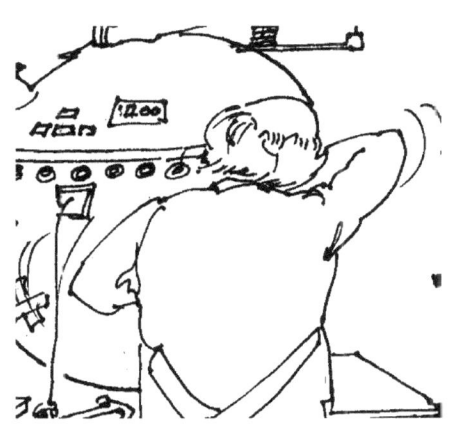

The boy thought, "That Amazing Person is just like the other champions. He's made a million more mistakes in inventing than most people have, because he practices so much! But, he's going to be really pleased with himself when his machine finally works just the way he wants it to."

As soon as he got home, the boy practiced the piano some. When he played some notes wrong, he said to himself, "Let me hear it in my mind and feel what I would feel like to play that right."

After he did that, he tried again and again and again. And after a while he could play it right about nine out of ten times. When he got it right, he said to himself, "Hooray! I'm glad I kept trying."

A few days later, the boy saw the Amazing Person again. The Amazing Person said, "Guess what! I got my machine working perfectly. Want to see?"

The amazing person said, "Let's tune in on a soccer player. Here he is practicing running and kicking the ball. As you can see, he makes lots of mistakes.

The Boy Learns About Champions' Mistakes

The boy was amazed to see that the soccer player on the screen was himself! The boy said to the Amazing Person, "Yes, that's just how it went only a day or two ago!"

The Amazing Person said, "It took me three hundred and forty-two more tries since I saw you last before I could get this thing working right! But boy, does it feel good to have done it!"

The boy could see that the Amazing person felt good, and the boy felt good too.

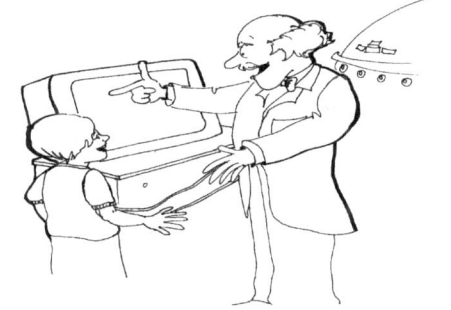

Cindy and the Scary Bedtime Problem

Going to bed at night was no fun for Cindy. As soon as she would go to her bedroom alone, she would become scared and start to worry.

She knew that robbers could not get into her house, but still she worried that a robber would come and get her.

When Cindy did fall asleep, she usually had scary dreams. Once she dreamed of a giant bird chasing her.

Cindy and the Scary Bedtime Problem

She also dreamed of a skeleton chasing her.

Cindy knew these scary things were not real. She knew that they were her own thoughts, but they still scared her. Most of the time, she'd go into her parents' bedroom and sleep on the floor in her sleeping bag.

One morning, Cindy's mother said to her, "Cindy, you're going to need to figure out a way to sleep in your own room. I hope you can do it."

"Try to stay in your own room at night. Each time you come out of your room, we'll put an X on the chart and just take you back to your bed. We won't talk to you."

Illustrated Stories That Model Psychological Skills

Cindy's father said, "If you can stay in your own bed all night without coming out, you get a great big star on your chart and we will clap in the morning and say, "Hooray for Cindy!"

Cindy said, "Maybe I won't be able to go to sleep. Should I stay in my own room anyway?"

Cindy's mother said, "That's right. You can get up and read. Or you can lie in bed and relax all night long without sleeping. It's all fine as long as you stay in your room without anyone's having to come to you."

Cindy wanted very much to be able to stay in her own room and not be scared. But she didn't know how she was going to do it. She walked along and wondered to herself.

Cindy and the Scary Bedtime Problem

Then Cindy saw Mr. James coming up the sidewalk carrying two big bags. Cindy liked Mr. James a lot. She waved to him and said, "Hi Mr. James!"

Mr. James said, "Hi, Cindy! I don't have a free hand, so I'll wave to you with my foot."

Cindy said, "Mr. James, why don't we carry those bags with my wagon? It'll be a lot easier."
Mr. James said, ""Cindy, that's a wonderful idea; I couldn't have thought of a better one myself." And they put the bags in Cindy's wagon.

As they walked along, Mr. James said, ""Cindy, you look like you have something on your mind. Do you want to tell me?"
Cindy said, "Yes, I've been trying to figure out how not to be scared at night when I go to bed."

Illustrated Stories That Model Psychological Skills

Mr. James said, "Well, you're lucky, Cindy. I happen to know a lot about how not to be scared at bedtime. You're so smart, I'll bet you can learn in only one lesson. Do you want one?"

Cindy wanted a lesson very much, so they sat down right there. Cindy told him about all the things that scared her, and Mr. James told her all sorts of wondrous things. They were talking so hard, they forgot all about Mr. James's groceries.

By the time Cindy said good-bye to Mr. James, she had decided that she knew how to do what she wanted to do.

Cindy went back to her bedroom and lay on her bed. She knew that she needed to practice thinking about some stories! The first story was to be called, "Cindy and the Robber."

Cindy and the Scary Bedtime Problem

This story started out with Cindy letting a make-believe robber into the house. She said, "Hi Robber! Welcome to our house!"

The robber looked confused. He said, "How did I get in here?" Cindy said, "I brought you here. I can do that, see, because you're part of my make-believe."
The robber said, "Uh, OK, well, if you say so, Cindy."

They sat down to have a chat. Cindy said, "Mr. Robber, why do you like to rob people?"
Mr. Robber said, "Well, I really don't like it very much. It's hard sneaking around so much at night. I step in holes, and too many dogs bark at me. I'd rather be home reading a good book."

Cindy said, "Well, if you'd rather be home, why do you rob?"
Mr. Robber said, "It's because I get hungry. I have to come in and rob people to get something to eat."

Cindy said, "Well, that's no problem. I'll give you something to eat. Come on." The make-believe robber looked happy to hear this.

Cindy made sure that the robber washed his hands before he ate.

Then she taught the robber to say the blessing.

Cindy gave him some strawberry shortcake. Then she said, "If you eat all your strawberry shortcake, you get to have some spinach and mushrooms!"
The robber said, "Hooray! Spinach and mushrooms are my favorite foods."

Cindy and the Scary Bedtime Problem

Then Cindy fixed him another very favorite food of his, which was a vanilla milk shake with a little bit of mashed potatoes mixed in with it!

Cindy said to him, "You can have this here, but you must remember not to order it in a restaurant. People will think you're strange if you do." The robber was interested to hear this, and he made a note of it in his notebook.

It was getting to be the robber's bedtime. But before he left, Cindy said to him, "I have a present for you before you go." And she gave him a magic pot of dirt and some seeds.

This pot and these seeds will let you grow spinach and mushrooms very fast so you can have them at any time. That way you won't have to rob people any more. But come back and see me again anyway."

Illustrated Stories That Model Psychological Skills

The robber thanked Cindy. Then he said, "I have a present for you, Cindy. It's a picture of me with my family."

Cindy said good-bye to the make-believe robber. And that was the end of the first story.

Cindy went outside and rode her bike. She looked forward to going back into her bedroom and having another story go through her mind.

After a while, Cindy went back inside and lay on her bed again. Now a new story came into her mind. It was called, "Cindy Meets the Skeleton and the Giant Bird."

Cindy and the Scary Bedtime Problem

In this story, Cindy said, "I'm going into my dreamland and meet a giant bird and a skeleton. Who wants to go with me? I'll need good friends."
Right away, a make believe Mr. James said, "I'll go with you."

Just as they were about to leave for Cindy's dreamland, another friend stepped up. "I want to go too," he said. It was Cindy's friend the robber. Cindy said, "Robber! I'm glad to see you!"
He said, "I used to be a robber, but now you can call me Ex-robber."

With that, they all sailed off to Cindy's dreamland.

When they arrived in Cindy's dreamland, the first thing they saw was a giant bird. The giant bird said, "Awk! Awk! How about if I pick you up and drop you in the lake, Cindy?"

Cindy said, "That sounds like fun, but my friends and I will have to check some things to make sure it is safe." The ex-robber put some foam on the bird's teeth so that they wouldn't tear Cindy's bathing suit.

They all changed into their swimming suits, while Mr. James checked to make sure the water didn't have hidden rocks in it.

So when all was safe, the giant bird took Cindy and flew out over the lake. Cindy got a great view.

Just at the right spot, the giant bird dropped Cindy into the lake. Cindy shouted out, "Whee!" as she dropped through the air. She did a flip on the way down.

Cindy and the Scary Bedtime Problem

The water was nice and warm. Cindy yelled out, "Thanks, Giant Bird." The giant bird gave her friends a nice ride out into the lake, too.

They swam toward the bank. When Cindy got a little tired, her friends towed her.

They got out of the lake, got dressed again, and decided to go for a walk. Just as they entered a deep dark wood, someone in a skeleton suit jumped out and said, "Book! I mean Boot! No, what I mean to say is Boo!"

Cindy and Mr. James and the ex-robber were not scared by the person in the skeleton suit. But they didn't want to hurt his feelings. Cindy said, "Boy, you sure do have a nice skeleton suit. I'll bet you scare a lot of people in that, huh?"

The person in the skeleton suit said, "Yes, but I see that I don't scare you. There are just too many of you. You've got me outnumbered. But that's OK. I'm just glad you didn't run away from me. I get kind of lonesome when people run away from me. When they run away, I don't have anyone to play with or talk to."

Cindy said, "You can come along with us! That way you won't be lonely. We can help and protect each other."
The person in the skeleton suit said, "Thank you. That would be great!"

All of a sudden, the giant bird flew out of the sky again. Cindy said, "Hi, giant bird! That was a fun swim, but I don't want to take another one."
The giant bird said, "That isn't what I had in mind. I came to get your help. My little baby giant bird is sick."

Cindy said, "Out of all these friends, maybe one of us knows something about doctoring sick animals."
The ex-robber said, "Yes, I can doctor animals. I've been studying to be a vet ever since I quit being a robber."

Cindy and the Scary Bedtime Problem

So the giant bird took them all to where she lived.

The baby giant bird was lying in bed. The ex-robber did some doctoring and Cindy and the rest of her friends helped out.

They did a good job of doctoring. Pretty soon, the baby giant bird was well! The mother giant bird was very happy.

And that was the end of the trip to Cindy's dreamland.

Cindy got up from bed. She thought, "Now the giant bird and the ex-robber and the person in the skeleton suit are my friends. I can have some fun with them in my dream tonight when I go to sleep."

Cindy went outside and rode her bike some more. She went to play with some real-life friends.

When bedtime came, Cindy kissed her father and mother goodnight. They told her again about the chart, even though she remembered it perfectly.

When Cindy went to bed, she was excited, but she wasn't very scared. She lay on her bed, closed her eyes, and started making up stories about her make-believe friends.

Cindy and the Scary Bedtime Problem

The ex-robber, the giant bird, and the person in the skeleton suit were just as friendly and nice as they had been earlier in the day. The make-believe Mr. James was in the story too.

After a while, the story turned into a good dream and Cindy slept.

The next morning when Cindy came to breakfast, there was a big star on the chart. Her mother and father were cheering for her.

Mr. James stopped in to say Hi. Cindy's mother said, "Mr. James, Look what Cindy did last night."

After that, they all sat down and had some breakfast.

Cindy kept making stories in her mind. She solved her scary bedtime problem.

Appendix: Using These Stories to Teach Sixteen Skills and Principles

It is very useful for a child to learn the vocabulary of psychological skills. Learning these words helps the child classify situations by what skill the situation calls for, and to be more organized in gaining access to their own repertoire of positive coping skills. Below is a list of sixteen skills and principles that make up mental health, with a short definition of each. For each story in this book, after the child reads it, the child can practice deciding which of two skills the story gives a more prominent example of. Many of the stories give examples of more than one skill. In the pairs of skills for each story that I have furnished as questions, I've tried to contrast one skill that the story does illustrate with one that the story does not particularly illustrate. You phase the question, for example, "Do you think that this story gives an example of honesty, or fortitude?"

Of course, before asking such questions, you have to teach the child what the words mean. If you want to use the stories to do this, you may say things like, "This story was an example of honesty. It was honest of her to give the money back rather than keep it for herself." Or: this story is an example of friendship-building. He made friends with the other boy when he came up and started talking with him and started playing with him." Then when you go back and read the story again, you can perhaps ask the question rather than say the answer.

Another of many steps in teaching these principles is to observe the child's real-life behavior, to note the positive examples, and to refer to them by these words, as in "Hey, nice productivity!" and "I know you wanted that, but you couldn't get it. You handled it well! You used some good fortitude skills!"

Here are the sixteen skills and principles:

1. Work hard. (productivity)
2. Be cheerful. (joyousness)
3. Be kind. Make people happy. (kindness)
4. Tell the truth. (honesty)
5. When you don't get what you want, handle it. (fortitude)

Illustrated Stories That Model Psychological Skills

6. Think carefully about what to do. (good decisions) Talk calmly when you don't agree with someone. (good decisions, conflict-resolution)
7. Don't hurt or kill. (nonviolence)
8. Don't use hurtful talk. (respectful talk, not being rude)
9. Build good relations with people. (friendship building)
10. Choose long term goals over short-term pleasure. (self-discipline)
11. Stick by people who have been good to you. (loyalty)
12. Don't waste the earth's resources. (conservation)
13. Take care of yourself. (self-care)
14. Obey when it is good and right to obey. (compliance)
15. In your fantasy, practice doing good things. Don't have fun pretending people are hurt. (positive fantasy rehearsal)
16. Be brave enough to do what's best. (courage)

Here are questions for the stories. (Numbers after the titles are page numbers for the stories.)

Sheila Gives the Money Back 7 : honesty or fortitude?
Jack Pets the Dog 10 kindness or nonviolence?
Toby Plays with a Lonesome Boy 13 self-discipline or friendship building?
Timmy and Matthew Take Turns 15 honesty or good-decisions (conflict resolution)?
Larry Keeps Sitting 18 self-discipline or courage?
Don Helps His Mother 21 productivity or self-care?
Mary Had a Good Time Anyway 24 fortitude or friendship-building?
Rusty Forgives Lunk 27 nonviolence or productivity?
Eddie Helps Maureen 30 conservation or kindness?
Bill Ignores Clint 33 nonviolence or productivity?
Bill Shares the Banana 36 nonviolence or kindness?
Jerry Helps the Child Out of the Water 38 courage or self-discipline?
James Helps Clara 41 kindness or self-discipline?
Cathy Says Something Nice 43 friendship-building or self-discipline?
Gwen Helps Jimmy 46 joyousness or kindness?
Myrna Helps the Boy Get Some Water 49 kindness or nonviolence?
Gina Helps Nancy 52 loyalty or kindness?
Brian Plays with Puppets 55 joyousness or courage?
Sherry Shares Her Doll 59 friendship-building or nonviolence?
Ted Gives His Seat to an Old Man 62 kindness or productivity?
Rusty Helps Push Cars 64 productivity or honesty?
Zeke Helps the Boys Fly the Kite 67 kindness or self-discipline?

Appendix: Using These Stories to Teach Sixteen Skills and Principles

Rusty Fixes the Boy's Bicycle 70 productivity or self-discipline?
Gina Helps Her Dog 72 compliance or good decisions?
Tony and Diane 74 good decisions (conflict-resolution) or courage?
Jane Gives a Greeting Card 77 honesty or kindness?
Richard Helps Michael 80 friendship-building or self-care?
Helen and the Strawberries 83 honesty or fortitude?
Amy Doesn't Let What People Say Bother Her 86 fortitude or compliance?
Alex Lets Jimmy Ride on the Bicycle 89 fortitude or good decisions?
Rusty Helps Tommy Learn to Swim 92 kindness or conservation?
Margo Feeds the Birds 96 courage or kindness?
Charlie Helps His Brother 99 respectful talk or nonviolence?
Louis Fastens the Seat Belt 102 joyousness or self-care?
The Witch and the Wizard Talk Out Their Problem 105 good decisions (conflict resolution) or self-care?
Hank Doesn't Get to Go to the Zoo 107 compliance or fortitude?
Kenny and Jerry and the Alligators 111 compliance or honesty?
Jan Tells Her Brother a Story 114 fortitude or kindness?
Linda Takes Care of Her Baby Doll 118 positive fantasy rehearsal or courage?
Jason Tames the Horse 122 conservation or friendship-building?
Maurice Shows a Book to a New Boy 125 friendship-building or nonviolence?
Jean Comforts Her Baby Sister 127 self-care or kindness?
The Boy and the Video Machines 130 courage or fortitude?
Michael Gives Back the Magic Wand 133 honesty or nonviolence?
Larry and the Monkey 137 respectful talk or good decisions?
The Man and the Lion 140 loyalty or self-discipline?
Mr. Monster Helps Mrs. Monster 144 self-care or kindness?
Lucia Helps Her Mother Change the Baby's Diapers 147 honesty or productivity?
Helen and Her Brother 150 kindness or self-discipline?
Brian Sees the Glove 153 respectful talk or self-discipline?
Teddy and His Resting Mother 156 good decisions or self-care?
Rusty Helps Timmy Fetch His Dog 158 kindness or compliance?
Lester Helps the Jumping Elf 161 conservation or kindness?
Maggie and Mrs. Robinson 165 friendship-building or productivity?
Joe and Larry Get the Tree 168 honesty or friendship-building?
James Lind Does an Experiment 171 productivity or conservation?
Jack Saves the Man from Freezing 176 courage or honesty?
Jack Helps the People Keep Warm 181 self-discipline or kindness?
Paul Reads to His Mother 185 productivity or conservation?
Gina Forgives Her Brother 188 self-care or nonviolence?

Illustrated Stories That Model Psychological Skills

Mack Helps the Little Girl 191 kindness or honesty?
Jimmy and Rolf-Ola Uglyzit 194 courage or conservation?
Frank Stops to Think 197 friendship-building or good decisions?
The Boy Goes to the Amazing People's Party 200 fortitude or productivity?
The Girl Waits for the Deer 205 self-discipline or productivity?
Hal and the Contest at the Magic Kingdom 209 good decisions or courage?
Marilyn Becomes Friends with a Lonely Girl 215 honesty or friendship-building?
The Amazing Person Helps Amos Not To Break Things 220 positive fantasy rehearsal or nonviolence?
Amos Stops to Think 224 good decisions or joyousness?
Deborah Helps the Squirrel 228 kindness or compliance?
Harry Helps His Dog 233 compliance or good decisions?
The Boy and the Complicated Present 237 self-care or productivity?
The Boy and the Rattlesnake 240 courage or honesty?
Jeff and the Broken Cup 243 joyousness or honesty?
Sheila Gets Separated From Her Mother 246 good decisions or friendship-building?
Gina and the Gymnastics Meet 250 nonviolence or good decisions?
Alex Helps the Animals 254 productivity or fortitude?
The Girl Handles it When Her Friend Leaves 261 honesty or fortitude?
Jean Handles It When Patty Moves Away 264 conservation or fortitude?
Frank and Zane Go Running 268 self-discipline or honesty?
Freddy and the Explosive 271 compliance or positive fantasy rehearsal?
James Lets the Little Boy Play With the Basketball 274 friendship-building or nonviolence?
George and the One-Way Street 277 good decisions or productivity?
Judy Makes a Plan About Her Dog 280 nonviolence or good decisions?
Peter and His Grandmother 283 loyalty or nonviolence?
The Boy and His Bow and Arrows 288 compliance or friendship-building?
The Boy and the Football 293 friendship-building or productivity?
Ted Waits for His Friends to Finish Playing 295 self-discipline or courage?
The Boy Who Could Put Up With His Parents' Paying Attention to Something Else 299 fortitude or honesty?
The Boy Learns About Champions' Mistakes 305 fortitude or respectful talk?
Cindy and the Scary Bedtime Problem 318 honesty or courage?

Appendix: Using These Stories to Teach Sixteen Skills and Principles

Here are answers to these questions. (A stands for the first answer mentioned above, and B stands for the second.)

Sheila A, Jack A, Toby B, Timmy B, Larry A, Don A, Mary A, Rusty A, Eddie B, Bill A, Bill B, Jerry A, James A, Cathy A, Gwen B, Myrna A, Gina B, Brian A, Sherry A, Ted A, Rusty A, Zeke A, Rusty A, Gina B, Tony A, Jane B, Richard A, Helen B, Amy A, Alex B, Rusty A, Margo B, Charlie A, Louis B, Witch A, Hank B, Kenny A, Jan B, Linda A, Jason B, Maurice A, Jean B, Boy B, Michael A, Larry B, Man A, Monster B, Lucia B, Helen A, Brian A, Teddy A, Rusty A, Lester B, Maggie A, Joe B, James Lind A, Jack A, Paul A, Gina B, Mack A, Jimmy A, Frank B, Boy A, Girl A, Hal A, Marilyn B, Amazing Person A, Amos A, Deborah A, Harry B, Boy B, Boy A, Jeff B, Sheila A, Gina B, Alex A, Girl B, Jean B, Frank A, Freddy A, James A, George A, Judy B, Peter A, Boy A, Boy A, Ted A, Boy A, Boy A, Cindy B

www.ingramcontent.com/pod-product-compliance
Lightning Source LLC
Chambersburg PA
CBHW081125170426
43197CB00017B/2756